Business Interruption, Supply Chain & Contingency

Didier Schütz (DLS)

Illustrated by Franck Orset (FPO)

Concepts, vulnerabilities, solutions, Risk Management perspectives

Business Interruption, Supply Chain & Contingency

© Didier Schütz (DLS) 2020

Preamble

"The most difficult subjects can be explained to the most slow-witted man if he has not formed any idea of them already; but the simplest thing cannot be made clear to the most intelligent man if he is firmly persuaded that he knows already, without a shadow of doubt, what is laid before him".
— Leo Tolstoy, 1897

I started to collect information about Business Interruption (BI), Contingent Business Interruption (CBI), Service Interruption (SI) and other related topics at the end of the 90's. My job of Loss Prevention Engineer for Direct Insurance and Re-Insurance gave me the opportunity to visit different industrial and commercial organizations worldwide.

I was trained together with a group of Western Europeans called "French Connection" (referring to a 1971 movie) at Kemper National long groove IL near Chicago. Thanks to my teachers, Bill Thomas and Scott Grieb, who gave me solid foundations, I acquired the taste to learn in a structured way. I'm still learning something every day.

The job of Loss Prevention Engineer consists of identifying and assessing risks and submitting prevention and protection recommendations. The protection will involve investment (i.e. automatic fire protection), where such recommendations should be economically justified by calculating the financial consequences resulting from the loss with and without protection. Assessing the risk also includes the calculation of the loss corresponding to the worst case scenario for insurance purposes as requested by the insured in order to set up their insurance cover limit and for (Re)insurers to assess their exposure. The loss expectancy for a given scenario is calculated in terms of **Property Damages (PD)** and **Business Interruption (BI)**.

Every time there is a big industrial event or a natural event impacting one or more industrial and commercial sectors, people tend to re-discover these concepts as if it were for the first time.

Business Interruption and supply chain related topics are not obvious because they are usually neither well understood nor adequately used. BI and supply chain concepts are not complicated, they are just over sophisticated and drowned in buzz words. At the end of the day this is not rocket science. No need to have specials skill to understand. It is better to have a good, comprehensive and clear cut explanation.

I have tried my best to clarify all these concepts and their mechanisms based on my proper experience. Thanks to Franck Orset (FPO) member of the "French Connection" for agreeing to illustrate this document.

From a Risk Management standpoint insurance cover is not the only answer to the interruption of business. This is just part of the answer needed for the insured to survive before resuming business. In case of a major loss an organization has much more to lose than what is paid out by the insurance.

In a global connected world, an organization may suffer a loss due to an event occurring very far away in another part of the world. Good understanding and preparedness as to what may cause an interruption shows the ability of an organization to manage its business in the face of uncertainty. Being able to expect the unexpected is the key to being adaptable.

The 2020 lockdown was global, impacting both businesses of any organizations and supply chains worldwide. Some people were speaking about a new era that would emerge after this period making our society more robust and resilient.

Content

1. INTRODUCTION	11
1.1. The Russian Dolls Concept	11
1.2. Growing interest / concerns /threats	12
1.2.1. Etymology of Business	12
1.2.2. Origin of Business	13
1.2.3. Business Growing with Inventions	14
1.3. The "ZOOG" Cocktail	16
1.4. Case Study – Western Automotive Manufacturers	23
2. BUSINESS OPERATING WINDOWS & INTERRUPTION	25
2.1. A world of Interaction	25
2.2. Operating Windows	25
2.3. Interruption	27
2.4. Example - Pandemic	28
2.5. Example – Oil Depot	30
3. MAIN ACRONYMS & TERMINOLOGY IN USE	35
3.1. The Alphabet Soup	35
3.2. From a (Re-)Insurance Perpective	35
3.3. Note on "Contingency"	37
4. BUSINESS INTERRUPTION (BI) FOCUS	39
4.1. BI Insurance	39
4.2. BI Effective Downtime	40
4.3. BI Financial Structure	42
4.4. BI as per Business Type	43

4.4.1.	Nominal BI	44
4.4.2.	Delay in Start Up (DSU) / Advanced Loss Of Profit (ALOP)	47

4.5. BI Trends — 48

4.6. BI Volatility — 53

4.7. BI as per Insurance Wording — 54
    4.7.1. BI Components — 55
    4.7.2. Main types of BI cover — 56
    4.7.3. Other costs that may be associated to BI: — 58

4.8. Sub-Product BI or Derivate BI — 58
    4.8.1. Cogeneration — 58
    4.8.2. Carbon Credit — 60

4.9. BI Assessment — 61

4.10. BI Loss Estimate — 69

5. INTERDEPENDENCIES (INDUCED BI) FOCUS — 71

5.1. Mutually Reliant on Each Other — 71

5.2. Induced BI as Downstream BI accumulation — 72

5.3. Induced BI as Upstream Extra Costs — 73

5.4. Induced BI as Extra Costs per Event — 73

6. CONTINGENT BUSINESS INTERRUPTION (CBI) FOCUS — 77

6.1. CBI Insurance Basics — 77

6.2. CBI Insurance Across the World — 77

6.3. Understanding CBI Insurance Cover — 78
    6.3.1. Governing perils — 78
    6.3.2. Limits consideration — 80
    6.3.3. Typically, CBI Insurance is NOT a — 81
    6.3.4. Strange CBI Insurance cover — 82

6.4. Supply Chain Vs CBI — 82
   6.4.1. CBI Contributing Property — 83
   6.4.2. CBI Recipient Property — 86
   6.4.3. CBI Leader Property — 86

6.5. CBI Impact — 88

6.6. CBI Tiers Factor — 89

6.7. CBI (Re)Insurance Purpose — 90
   6.7.1. The fire that changed the Industry — 90
   6.7.2. The goldfish syndrome — 93
   6.7.3. Stress Test for the Global economy — 94
   6.7.4. Need for Managing CBI Accumulation — 96
   6.7.5. CBI Claims development — 97

7. SERVICE INTERRUPTION (SI) FOCUS — 99

7.1. SI Definition — 99

7.2. SI Loss Magnitude — 100

7.3. SI Insurance needs — 102

7.4. SI Insurance Across the World — 103

7.5. Understanding SI Insurance Cover — 103
   7.5.1. Extent of coverage — 103
   7.5.2. Governing Perils — 105
   7.5.3. Limits consideration — 106

7.6. SI Loss Experiences — 108

8. OTHER BI EXTENSION FOCUS — 113

8.1. Increased Vs Additional Increase in - Cost of Working — 113

8.2. Alternative Accommodation — 118

8.3. Loss of Rent — 119

8.4. Contingency Extension — 119

8.5. Prevention of Access — 120

8.6. Action of Competent Authorities — 122

8.7. Loss of Attraction	128
8.8. "CBI No Damage"	129
8.9. Potpourri	130
9. OTHER BI RELATED CONSEQUENCES	**133**
9.1. Induced Financial Consequences following a loss	133
9.2. Loss of market Share	134
9.3. Loss of Reputation	135
9.4. Other	137
10. BUSINESS INTERRUPTION & CONTINGENT BI MITIGATION	**139**
10.1. Breaking the Myth of Confidence	139
10.2. Understanding the Interactions	145
10.3. Establishing a Resilience Strategy	**149**
10.3.1. Favorite Weapons (CP, BCP/M)	149
10.3.2. Reliability Issue (CP, BCP/M)	151
10.3.3. When to consider a CP as reliable	151
10.3.4. CP, BCP/M for Supply Chain	155
10.3.5. CP, BCP/M generating Business Opportunity	159
10.3.6. Norms, Standards and Certification	160
10.3.7. Expect the unexpected	161
10.3.8. Aware, Adaptive, Associate	163
10.4. Financing BI/CBI Residual Risk	169
11. RECOMMENDED BOOKS	**173**

1. INTRODUCTION

1.1. The Russian Dolls Concept

It would be nonsensical to speak about Contingent Business Interruption (CBI) or even Business Interruption (BI) without first speaking about the foundations of these somehow sophisticated or advanced concepts from the (Re-)Insurance perspective.

As a result of the above and to better our understanding, let's go back to typical insurance cover arrangements and mechanisms:
- A Property insurance policy only covers the physical damage to the business (i.e. Property Damage).
- Business Interruption (BI) insurance (also known as business income insurance) is a type of insurance that covers the loss of income that a business suffers after a disaster. BI coverage can be added onto the business' Property insurance policy (above) or the comprehensive package policy such as a business owner's policy (BOP).
- A Contingent Business Interruption insurance policy is a type of insurance that provides benefits if earnings are reduced because of damages to another business on which one's own is dependent. Contingent business interruption (CBI) insurance is therefore an extension to other insurance policies (i.e. Property, Business Interruption above) that reimburses lost profits and extra expenses resulting from an interruption of business at the premises of a customer or supplier or even of a so called "leader property" (third party attracting customers and/or providing services as part of the business). In some jurisdictions there is a dedicated coverage for the failure of utilities which is called "Service Interruption" instead of CBI.

Since BI is included as part of the business' primary policy (Property cover), it only pays out if the cause of the loss is covered by the overarching policy. Same principles apply for the CBI on top of BI cover. At the end of the day CBI is an extension of BI and BI is an extension of Property cover. Other contingent extensions (see dedicated section) may also be added. This arrangement looks like "Russian Dolls" (Matryoshka), the Property cover being the main "trigger" for the other covers to apply:

Property Cover (PD) — Business Interruption (BI) — Contingent Business Interruption (CBI) — Service Interruption (SI) — Contingency Extension

© Franck Orset (FPO)

Note: BI and CBI can be part of a standalone policy in some jurisdictions. These covers only pay out if the cause of the loss is a defined event. These standalone policies are not as common as the general case described above.

1.2. Growing interest / concerns /threats

1.2.1. Etymology of Business

Any business can be a source of extreme and inextricably linked feelings that are a mixture of both excitement and fear, probably the result of taking risks and managing the business in the face of uncertainty. The etymology may provide the beginning of an explanation:

- From Old English (mid-5th century): bisignes (Northumbrian) "care, anxiety, occupation," from bisig "careful, anxious, busy, occupied, diligent".
- From Middle English (after the Norman conquest in 1066 until the late 15th century): busines, busynes, businesse, bisynes.

The original sense (Old English) is obsolete, as is the Middle English sense of "state of being much occupied or engaged" (mid-14c.), the latter replaced by busyness.

1.2.2. Origin of Business

The first businesses can be traced back to nearly 20,000 years ago. Hunter-gatherer tribes trading tools, food, skins from different parts of their respective regions to provide an overall benefit for their tribe.

The first major business shift took place during the Agricultural Revolution about 12,000 years ago starting with the settlement of nomads in villages and then towns. Farmers handled food production while the rest of the population focused on other tasks. This was the first step towards specialization. The overall benefit was limited to the villages or the towns.

From 2000 BC on, trade started to develop between towns and cities.

Money was invented in 200 BC using seashells, tobacco leaves, beads, rocks, etc.

Larger marketplaces for larger populations were developed during the medieval period.

In the second half of the 15th century important developments took place in terms of banking solutions for financing business projects, regulation of the quality of goods, purchasing goods from abroad and processing goods into finished products.

The philosophy of mercantilism was basically born with the exploration of the new world from 1550 to 1800. Standardized principles for keeping track of a firm's accounts were established.

The Industrial Revolution started in the 18th century and consisted of a major switch from small-scale production in small towns to large-scale production in big cities, thus, involving the production of energy such as electricity and steam and oil for machines. The need for labor led to huge populations moving to bigger cities. The demand for manufactured goods increased due to new markets.

The economy became more global after World War II because of better ways of shipping and means of communication.

Today, the global economy is combined with modern infrastructure and communications, and businesses are interacting all over the world.

New challenges include the access to energy and raw materials, labor costs, processing technologies and regulations.

1.2.3. Business Growing with Inventions

The following periods, milestones and main inventions are summarized below:

Industrial Revolution 1800-1840 AC
- World population: 978 million
- Steam, steamboats departing from the UK to NY
- Electrolysis
- Gas lighting in London and Paris
- Textile trade

Machinery 1840-1855
- Synthetic Fertilizer manufacturing
- Rotating press
- 1st Great Exhibition in London: Crystal Palace
- Paris' massive urban renewal program - Haussmann
- Cook travel: organized trips

Konzern (group) 1860-1880
- Darwin: origin of species
- Mendel: basics of genetics
- Abolition of slavery
- Workers' unions foundation

Steel – Electricity: 1880-1900
- Skyscraper (steel structure), Eiffel Tower (1890)
- Electric power station at Niagara Falls
- Electrification of cities
- Mass production
- The Belle Epoque - Les frères lumières (cinema)

Transportation 1900-19120
- World population: 1.65 billion
- Automotive mass production
- Trans-Siberian Railway
- Titanic
- The First World War

Rationalization 1920-1935
- The Roaring Twenties (Le Corbusier)
- Booming of oil production in the US
- 15 million Ford T's produced
- The Great Depression of 1929)

Automation 1940-1955
- The Second World War: 55 million dead
- 90% of road accidents caused by technical failure
- Invention of radar (origin of computer and microwave)
- First robots
- Nuclear technology

Communication 1960-1980
- Cold War - Space Conquest - Satellites
- Silicon Valley - Multimedia
- Plastic products
- Mass tourism
- Oil shocks - Ozone Hole - Alternative Energy

Globalization 1980 – 2000
- World population : 6.16 billion
- Glasnost (openness) and Perestroika (restructuring) of the USSR
- Star Wars (US- Reagan)
- Tchernobyl civil nuclear event
- 90% of road accidents caused by humans
- Internet - virtual-biotechnology - nanotechnology
- Global Players

1.3. The "ZOOG" Cocktail

From the 1980s on, business was boosted by a set of practices that mainly aimed at improving efficiency and reducing costs. This can be summarized as the "ZOOG cocktail" as follows:

ZOOG Cocktail ingredients:
- **Zero Stock**
- **Optimization**
- **Outsourcing**
- **Globalization**

Recipe:
- As much as you can
- Anywhere, ASAP
- No limits
- Shaken and or stirred. Who cares.

© Franck Orset (FPO)

Note: do not confuse this with other definitions that can be found in some dictionaries such as:
- Zoog is a name used for a person who has blond hair, who is really weird, and smokes a lot of weed.
- Some examples: "john: look at that dude over there!; Sam: ha-ha yeah he is such a typical zoog".

The components of the ZOOG cocktail are described below:

- **Zero Stock**: the goal is to limit the amount of goods stored on site to a minimum. It applies first to Raw Materials, Work In Progress materials (including buffer storage, Finished Products) and also to Spare Parts (consumable, critical), Packaging Materials and Furniture.

    Zero Stock can also be assimilated to the concept of "**Just In Time**", thus, leading to very interesting situations that may even compromise the Continuity Plan (CP):

    Example 1 - an aluminum smelter in the Gulf using alumina as a raw material having 120,000 tons capacity in 2 silos on site (in-built CP). This is sufficient for providing 30 days production in case of a supply chain disruption (e.g. supplier issue, storm, single un-loader impaired at port facility, etc.). This stock was later reduced to 45,000 tons to reduce capital lock-in (less than 12 days' supply corresponding to the monthly ship load coming from Australia to Middle East)

Example 2 – automotive industry assembling 400 cars a day involving multiple components delivered by contractors including a USD 5 fuel valve. The buffer stock on site corresponds to only 4 hours car manufacturing and the valves are delivered by truck every 4 hours. This results in a very tense supply chain.

For some organizations this also necessitates a serious change in production philosophy from:

- "**Work to Store**" (such as wine produced and kept for maturation of the product)

to

- "**Work on Order**" (e.g. production of mass communication systems – mobile phones – having a very short life span on the market. A production line is set-up and components are purchased from the market to manufacture a certain type of phone upon order from a customer).

Depending on the type of Finished Products some industry sectors have developed both "working styles".

Example – an integrated Steel Mill :

Plant A: Rod bars for the construction sector are mass produced and are regularly manufactured, stored on site and sold on the market. Inventory is therefore subject to important variations depending on market demand (i.e. Work to store)

Plant B: Heavy Section products (i.e. heavy beams) also for the construction sector are products made to order for a specific use (i.e. the frame of a building). Some mill equipment is entirely dedicated to the making of these products.

- **Optimization**: This is a multi-component practice including:
  - **Rationalization**. Thus, applying to production equipment but also to the supply chain:

    Instead of having multiple production lines for the same product (thus, giving flexibility and back up) a single processing line with higher capacity is installed.

    Instead of having multiple sources of Raw Material (as part of the Contingency Plan) a sole supplier is chosen, thus allowing for a reduction in the cost of Raw Materials because of higher quantities negotiated with the supplier.

  - **Concentration**: very similar to rationalization above but applying at the level of a plant or a site instead of a production line. The purpose is to avoid any duplication within a group, having one plant specialized in the manufacturing of a dedicated product instead of having multiple sites manufacturing the same products. This leads to a high level of specialization of a plant or a site. A plant can only be specialized in one of the process steps for manufacturing a good so that the final product is in fact a Work In Progress material or semi-finished product to be processed in the next plant. This gives rise to very important interdependencies between sister plants belonging to the same manufacturing group.

  - **Integration**: There are 3 main types of integration:

    Vertical Integration: the merging together of two businesses which are at different stages of production. The merge can also include a supplier for fuel / water / electricity (i.e. so-called "life line" or utilities).

    Example 1: a food manufacturer and a chain of supermarkets. Merging in this way with something further on in the production process (and thus closer to the final consumer) is known as forward integration.

    Example 2: a group of farmers in Montana purchasing a crude oil refinery in Canada for securing the supply of fuel oil / diesel oil in case of shortage on the market (so called independent Strategic Supply of Diesel and Fuel Oil).

Example 3: similar to example 2 but with a different goal. An airline based in the US buys a refinery to gain control of Jet A1 fuel costs to curb the impact of the high volatility of costs of hydrocarbon refined products (i.e. oil crisis, geo-politics, etc.).

Example 4: a group specialized in Aluminum business from mineral material mining (bauxite) to Alumina refining, Aluminum production (smelter) and downstream aluminum (Rolling Mill, cable factory, etc.). This results in total control of the supply chain for Raw Materials and Work In Progress material.

Example 5: an "integrated automotive manufacturing complex" in the Far East covers all production steps such as engine casting, body forming, plastic bumpers manufacturing, assembly, painting, testing. Only the rubber tires are supplied by a third party.

Horizontal Integration: Horizontal integration is the acquisition of a business operating at the same level of the value chain in a similar or different industry. A company may do this via internal expansion, acquisition or merger. The process can lead to a monopoly if a company captures the vast majority of the market for that product or service.

Example 1: food industry. A group producing various brands of cookies, chocolate and candies, pasta, rice based products, beverages.

Example 2: a media group including TV, radio, newspapers, web, etc.

Symbiosis: Industrial symbiosis is a form of brokering to bring companies together in innovative collaborations, finding ways to use the waste from one as raw material for another. Strategic planning is required to optimize the synergies of co-location. In practice, using industrial symbiosis as an approach to commercial operations - using, recovering and redirecting resources for reuse - results in resources remaining in productive use in the economy for longer. This in turn creates business opportunities, reduces demands on the earth's resources and provides a stepping-stone towards creating a circular economy.

Example: The Kalundborg Symbiosis in Denmark was developed in 1972. This is the World's first industrial symbiosis with a circular approach to production, a partnership between eleven public and private companies. The main principle is that a residue from one company becomes a resource at another, benefiting both the environment and the economy. Having a local partnership means that they can share and reuse resources, and that way they save money as well as minimize waste.

- **Automation**: most modern processes have a relatively high level of automation allowing for better efficiency and especially better quality. Automation systems include but are not just limited to Information Technology (IT), Human Machine Interfaces (HMI), Distributed Control Systems, Process Logical Controllers, robots, etc. Theoretically most of the processes can be run almost on manual mode using a local controller. However, it appears that manual mode production cannot last for a long period without reducing the quality and the production rate and without limiting the range of products. So manual mode is not sustainable on a middle – long term basis (usually cannot exceed a few weeks).

- **Sharp edge technology**: some technologies installed on a given plant require a license granted by the inventor (licensor). A manufacturing license agreement (MLA) is an agreement between an inventor and a manufacturer (i.e. a chemical process). The agreement allows a third party to produce and use the inventor's product for payment in royalties or a specific lump sum. In case of a technical issue with the process, the manufacturer may be very dependent on the licensor. Technical agreements for the maintenance, inspection but also on-line remote monitoring of some critical pieces of equipment (i.e. gas turbine) may also be required for the warranty to apply during the period after installation and sometimes there are not even any alternatives for taking care of the maintenance as the equipment ages. These sophisticated pieces of equipment usually have a long lead time (single Original Equipment Manufacturer). Some equipment needs to be sent back to the OEM located overseas for either repair or re-calibration.

- **Outsourcing**: Outsourcing is an agreement in which one company hires another company to be responsible for a planned or existing activity that is or could be done internally, and sometimes involves transferring employees and assets from one firm to another. The term outsourcing, which came from the phrase outside-resourcing, originated no later than 1981.

    The main purposes of outsourcing are:
    - Cost Reduction
    - Focus on Core
    - Improve quality
    - Increase speed to market
    - Foster Innovation
    - Conserve Capital

    This can include:
    - **Non-core business**: e.g. maintenance, inspection, load handling, catering, security, utilities, transportation, R&D for manufacturing spares (e.g. drawings and moulds are developed, owned, stored by the contractor).
    - **Core business**: production, operation (installation can be owned, maintained and operated by a third party – i.e. Air Separation Plant – or owned and maintained by the plant but operated by a third party.

    The main challenges in terms of outsourcing are the supervision and coordination.

- **Globalization**: Globalization is the spread of products, investment and technology across national borders and cultures. In economic terms, it describes the loosening of barriers to international trade thus allowing for:
    - Moving closer to Raw Materials / Customers, source of energy.
    - Networking.

- o Specialization of some countries (e.g. semiconductor R&D labs in Asia - Pacific).
- o Technology transfer.
- o Local manpower proficiency development.
- o Cost flexibility, Tax reduction, incentive creation.
- o Adaptive local regulation.
- o Fungibility: goods and assets are interchangeable - mutual substitution of goods & services.
- o Organization switches from multi-national to regional specialization & concentration.
- o Production moving to the new lowest cost country.

Warning: like any drug, the ZOOG cocktail may lead to some "addictions" and "side effects" as described below:

ACTIVE INGREDIENT	PURPOSE (Drug Facts)	WARNINGS (Side Effects)
Zero Stock	Efficient Just-in-time business (Storage & tax reduction)	Production Shut down in case of Shortage
Optimization	Reduction of production costs (automation - avoid redundancies, concentration)	Edge of technology, lack of back-up, high dependency. Loss of Flexibility
Outsourcing	Focus on core business with higher added value	Loss of Control of some process steps
Globalization	Production flexibility. Maximum fungibility of capital	Worldwide sensitivity to man-made perils & acts of god

1.4. Case Study – Western Automotive Manufacturers

Consolidation of the industry between 1988 and 2008:
- At the level of the Automotive Manufacturer: 23 major Companies in 1988 and only 12 left in 2008.
- At the level of the Suppliers: 600 major suppliers reported in 2001 versus 22 in 2008.

Major production changes:
- "Just-in-Time" type of production (no buffers to mitigate a disruption in production).
- High level of automation (higher vulnerability to failure of automatic process).
- Moving away from a single-mode mass production model to a more flexible manufacturing supply chain.
- Collaborative product development including more interactions between different business partners.
- Industry moving towards sub assembly modules, systems and platforms with key partners.

Example:
- A platform in Europe in charge of the final assembly of cars for various Automotive Manufacturers. Parts are received from Original Equipment Manufacturers – OEMs (companies that produce parts and equipment that may be marketed by another manufacturer).
- From a Risk Management standpoint: A major fire destroying or severely damaging the above platform would result in production disruption for various Automotive Manufacturers over Europe.
- In terms of (Re-)insurance this would lead to a major accumulation if the (Re-)insurer is involved with various other Automotive Manufacturers using the same platform (i.e. the sum of the various CBI limits would be above € 1 billion).

© Franck Orset (FPO)

2. BUSINESS OPERATING WINDOWS & INTERRUPTION

2.1. A world of Interaction

A modern organization is interacting with various internal stakeholders and external business partners, some of which may be:
- The corporation
- Suppliers
- Customers
- Retailers / Distribution
- E-marketplace / Portal
- Logistics
- Partners
- Manufacturers
- Authorities

These stakeholders, business partners and the ensuing interactions define an environment which can be divided into 3 main business operating windows as described below.

2.2. Operating Windows

The inner operating window represents the "Organization" comprising all operations and stakeholders belonging to the same entities such as corporate offices, so-called sister plants (e.g. belonging to the same group), distribution centers, retail centers and shops if any (depending on the level of vertical and horizontal integration).

Example below: a crude oil rig extracting oil to be processed in the crude oil refinery. Both oil rigs and refinery belong to the same legal entity. The organization basically has almost full control of this window (i.e. field of expertise, operating strategic decisions).

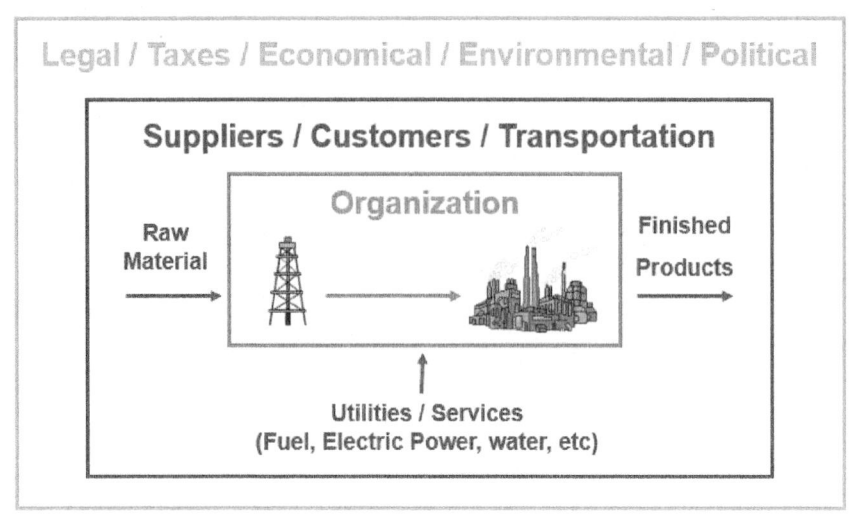

```
┌─────────────────────────────────────────────────────────┐
│   Legal / Taxes / Economical / Environmental / Political│
│   ┌─────────────────────────────────────────────────┐   │
│   │     Suppliers / Customers / Transportation       │   │
│   │   ┌───────────────────────────────────────┐     │   │
│   │   │          Organization                  │     │   │
│   │   │ Raw                          Finished │     │   │
│   │   │ Material    🛢  →  🏭       Products  │     │   │
│   │   │   →                             →      │     │   │
│   │   └───────────────────────────────────────┘     │   │
│   │                    ↑                              │   │
│   │           Utilities / Services                    │   │
│   │      (Fuel, Electric Power, water, etc)           │   │
│   └─────────────────────────────────────────────────┘   │
└─────────────────────────────────────────────────────────┘
```

© Didier Schütz (DLS)

The **middle operating window** represents all business partners that allow the "Organization" to run its business. This includes:

- The suppliers: supplying Raw Material(s) but also including spare parts, furniture, catering (especially for remote locations), etc. An example for the Organization as described above could be: additives and chemicals supplied by third party(ies) could be injected into the oil field for purposes of processing .

- The customers: receiving the Finished Products to be processed again in case of semi-finished products or even to be customized (e.g. trimming of metal sheets) or re-packaged and re-branded (e.g. receiving bulk cement to be sold in 25kg sacks under a local brand).

- Utilities and Service Providers: including all life lines such as fuel oil, gas, electric power, steam, drinkable / processing / cooling water, air products (i.e. Air Separation Plant - ASP), telecommunications (e.g. IT, Tel), specialized maintenance and technical support (e.g. Technical agreement for Gas Turbines), all outsourced activities such as security (watchman service), cleaning, fire-fighting services (private company), fire detection / protection maintenance, inspection and testing, consultant, accounting (payroll, factoring), leased / rented fleet of vehicles, repair garage facilities, load handling, transportation, etc.

The organization as described above would have some level of control of the middle operating window.

The outer operating window basically represents the wider environment where the business is taking place. This includes:
- The so-called "Authorities Having Jurisdiction" (AHJ): An entity, office, or individual responsible for enforcing the requirements of a code, standard, regulation or law. The AHJ may be international, national, federal, state, regional, local, etc. The definition of AHJ is fairly broad meaning that a given organization, such the one defined above, would have very little control over the decisions taken by the AHJ. Example: the use of some chemicals may be banned in some countries. Export of Finished Products may be subject to very prohibitive taxes, additional taxes on utilities or Value Added Taxes, taxes on foreign contractors to protect the local market, etc., local environmental regulations only allowing for very low emission levels, labor laws regulating overtime work. National accounting rules may be very different from country to country. Electric code is usually dedicated to a given country.
- The social, economic, financial, political, related natural events and even health conditions (local, regional, national, international). A given Organization such the one described above would basically have NO control on the decision taken by the AHJ Example: sanctions, war, oil shock, market dumping, lobbying, commodity / utility price speculation, (Re-)insurance soft/hard market conditions, "acts of god", air travel disruption (2010 eruption of Eyjafjallajökull in Iceland), Thailand flood in 2010 and Japan Earthquake & tsunami and Fukushima Nuclear Incident, worldwide health crisis (i.e. 2020 Covid19), weather changes, etc.

2.3. Interruption

For the operating windows above, an "Interruption" is anything that prevents an organization remaining in business, as detailed below:
- At the level of the inner operating window (Organization), an explosion at the oil rig would result in a shortage of crude oil to be processed at the refinery. In the case of a Vapor Cloud

Explosion at the refinery, the production of crude oil at the oil rig will have to stop.

- Within the **middle operating window** any failure of supplier, customer or utilities / service provider will have an impact on the business of the Organization (inner window). Example: due to the fire occurring at an Original Equipment Manufacturer, an automotive manufacturer will be forced to shut down a car production line (i.e. supply chain disruption).
- At the level of the outer operating window any event in this global and connected world may have an impact on the Organization (inner window). Example: sanctions taken against a country forcing a closure of the plants located in this country, or a Worldwide Pandemic involving strict lockdown of populations resulting in all plants shutting down.

Moreover, any event occurring in one operating window can have an impact on all the other windows as shown in the following example.

2.4. Example - Pandemic

© Franck Orset (FPO)

This example shows how an event generated in the outer operating window (i.e. pandemic) impacted both middle and inner operating windows.

The 2002–2004 SARS outbreak was an epidemic resulting in a severe acute respiratory syndrome (SARS) caused by the severe acute respiratory syndrome coronavirus (SARS-CoV or SARS-CoV-1). The outbreak was first identified in Foshan, Guangdong,

China, in November 2002. Over 8,000 people from 29 different countries and territories were infected and at least 774 died worldwide. The major part of the SARS outbreak lasted about 8 months, as the World Health Organization declared the severe acute respiratory syndrome contained on 5 July 2003. However, several SARS cases were reported until May 2004.

On September 29, 2005, the United Nations System Coordinator for Avian and Human Influenza (H5N1), warned the world that an outbreak of avian influenza could kill anywhere between 5 million and 150 million people.

The 2009 swine flu pandemic H1N1 lasted about 20 months, from January 2009 to August 2010 (600,000 dead reported worldwide). The impact of the swine flu pandemic H1N1 was reportedly relatively low outside Asia.

In 2019, the Corona Virus Disease (Covid-19) pandemic started in Asia. Many countries in Asia were the main producers of critical heath care material, equipment and drugs but had to supply their own countries first leaving them with basically no spare capacity for export.

In early 2020 when the health crisis spread to the rest of the world, several countries ran out of critical heath care material, equipment and chemicals for tests and drugs extremely quickly. Most production capacity had gradually been relocated to Asia during the previous decades and the supply from Asia was disrupted because of the on-going Covid-19 pandemic.

The only solution found by the government of most of these countries to contain the pandemic considering but not limited to the available capacity of the intensive care units was a total lockdown of the population for several weeks. The majority of the industries, transportation and commercial occupancies had, therefore, to stop their business in accordance with the administrative decision.

Covid-19 - Message from Denis Kessler, Chairman & CEO of SCOR SE (Global Tier-One Reinsurer) March 30, 2020: "The situation we are currently experiencing is unprecedented. The coronavirus pandemic has become a multifaceted crisis: sanitary, social, economic, financial and even geopolitical. The pandemic is the perfect example of the serial risk, unrestricted by space and time, to which our modern, globalized societies are particularly vulnerable".

2.5. Example – Oil Depot

This example shows how an event generated in the inner operating window (i.e. explosion in an oil depot) impacted both the middle and outer operating windows.

This tank farm is located about 40km of a capital city in Western Europe. This is the fifth largest oil tank farm in this country. It was built in 1960 on a 50 Ha ground area of which 8 kms is an industrial area.

The total capacity is of 100 000cum hydrocarbons in 39 tanks in 8 bunds. It is comprised of 2 loading stations (400 trucks per day) and 2 pipelines respectively linking the Northern part of the country and the main international airport.

At the time of the loss some weeks before Christmas in 2005, this oil depot was a multi-tenant facility involving various petroleum companies and a pipeline agency.

A massive escape of fuel from an 8,000cum Unleaded Gasoline Tank formed a flammable mixture with the air drifting eastwards before the flammable cloud was ignited resulting in an explosion.

Bund seals were damaged by fire and the hydraulic pressure of fuel causing fuel on fire to escape and the fire to spread within the site.

About 80% of the tank farm was destroyed. Result: Property damage.

Damages were about € 52 million for inventories and € 37 million for the tanks. The cost of water and ground decontamination was about € 10 million.

The nearest Industrial area employing 16,500 people adjacent to the Oil Depot site suffered a total direct economic impact amounting to € 145-190 million and many indirect impacts:
- 2,000 people evacuated.
- 70 schools damaged and closed.
- 88 businesses severely damaged.
- 20 Premises destroyed (employing 500 people).
- 60 premises needed repairing (employing 3,500 people).
- 4,000-5,000 jobs affected.
- Many companies were left non-operational or semi-operational (buildings safety assessments, restricted access).
- Some large companies were re-located (Social & Economic Impact).
- Loss of goods in local warehouses awaiting shipping (Christmas goods).
- Housing market: 300 houses damaged. Mostly minor damage to domestic property. Average claims from individual: # € 10,000.
- The Uncertain future of the Oil Depot continues to cause concern to local businesses, employees and residents.

Other unquantifiable impacts outside the Oil depot area include:
- Temporary outsourced payroll service disruptions.
- Temporary loss of the capital city traffic congestion charging administration.
- Perimeter roads obstructed and remote motorway sections (29km away) temporarily shut. Sections of the main motorways were closed.
- Short, mid, long-term environmental impacts (air, ground water, surface water, soil on-site / off-site), thus warranting the need for a long term monitoring and sampling program.

At the country level, this fifth most important oil tank farm in the country was a strategic important fuel storage site operated by a number of companies.
- The depot received petrol, aviation fuel, diesel and other fuels by pipeline.

- It stored, then distributed these fuels by pipeline and road tanker to the capital region and SE of the country:
  - This Oil Depot handled 8 % of overall country oil supplies on the market including 20% of supply to consumers of the SE region (120 Road tankers were on site at the time of the loss – Potential shortage).
  - The terminal acted as a main pipeline transit point to meet 40% of the main international airport's demand for Jet A1 (21 million litres per day consumption). The main international airport was temporarily closed due to the heavy smoke cloud. The event also resulted in temporary fuel rationing and loss of profit for the airport.

The estimated Oil Depot total quantifiable loss was close to € 1.1 billion of which:
- Site operators (compensation claims) € 695 million.
- Aviation € 270 million.

The Oil Depot explosion and fire event was deemed as one of the "Top 12" Industrial Fires since WWII in Peacetime Europe:
- 1948 Ludwigshafen, Germany: explosion of a tank wagon within BASF-site.
- 1965 Little Rock AFB, Searcy, Arkansas: fire at a Titan missile silo.
- 1974 Flixborough: explosion at a chemical plant.
- 1988 Norco, Louisiana, Shell Oil Refinery: Explosion of hydrocarbon gas. The total cost arising from the Norco blast is estimated at USD 706m.
- 1988 Auburn, Indiana: improper mixing of chemicals at a metal-plating plant
- 1988 Piper Alpha: explosion and resulting fire on a North Sea oil production platform killing 167 men. Total insured loss was about USD 3.4 billion.
- 1989 Phillips Pasadena, Texas: Explosion and fire.
- 1991 Hamlet chicken processing plant fire.
- 1993 Kader Toy Factory: fire.

- 2000 Enschede Netherlands fireworks depot: fire and explosion. The damage was estimated to be over USD 300 million in insured losses.
- 2005 Texas City Refinery: explosion due to overfilling of a knock out drum.

3. MAIN ACRONYMS & TERMINOLOGY IN USE

3.1. The Alphabet Soup

"Wall-street loves to use confusing terms, to make you think only they can do what they do."
Michael Lewis, The Big Short: Inside the Doomsday Machine

The same may happen with all acronyms and terms enclosed in this document:
- Business Interruption (BI)
- Interdependencies (Induced BI)
- Service Interruption (SI)
- Contingent Business Interruption (CBI)
- Contingent Time Element (CTE)
- Other BI Extensions (Contingency extensions)

3.2. From a (Re-)Insurance Perpective

Interruption of Business from an insurance perspective can be easily summarized as show on the previously described "operating windows" (see section 2.2) diagram below:

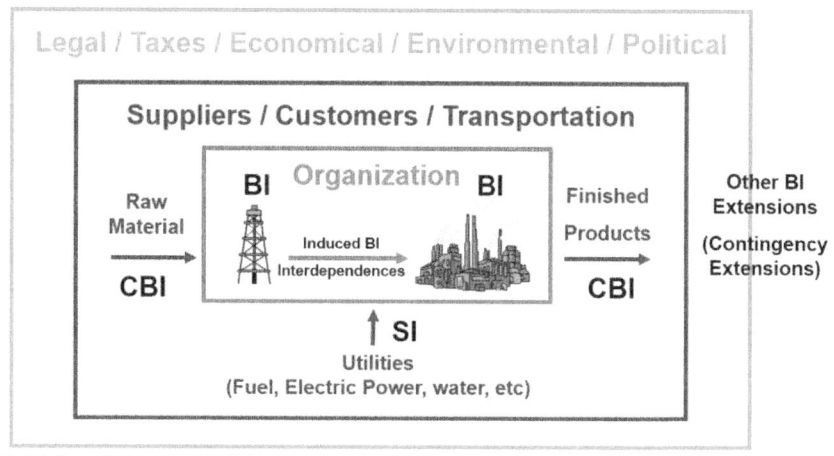

© Didier Schütz (DLS)

BI - Business Interruption: refers to any interruption of business originating inside the perimeter of a location (e.g. plant, warehouse, office, etc.) belonging to the "Organization". For example: a major fire occurring at the oil rig will result in Business Interruption of the oil rig.

Interdependences – Induced BI: refers to any business link between sister entities belonging to the same "Organization". When such business links exist between two entities A and B, a loss occurring at plant A producing semi-finished products to be processed at plant B will generate an "induced BI" at plant B (i.e. basically no Raw Material supplied from plant A which is the internal supplier of plant B). The same principle applies in the case of a major loss at plant B resulting in a shut down. Plant A will have to stop production due to the loss of its internal customer.
Note that semi-finished products can be referred to as Work in Progress (WIP) Material.
For example: An explosion at the oil rig will induce BI at the refinery due to the lack of crude oil supply from the oil rig.

CBI - Contingent Business Interruption: refers to any interruption of business suffered by the "Organization" due to the failure of its suppliers (for Raw Material) or customers (for Finished Products) located outside the "Organization". This is typically a rupture of in the supply chain caused by an event occurring outside the "Organization" (e.g. fire at the supplier or customer).
Note that the term CTE (Contingent Time Element) instead of CBI can be used (i.e. US market). CTE can also include any third party called "leader property" independent of the "Organization" but allowing / supporting the business of the "Organization" (e.g. a show room). (See CBI section for more details).
CBI does NOT usually include any utility such as power or water. This is part of SI below.

SI – Service Interruption: refers to any interruption of business suffered by the "Organization" due to the failure of its utilities / service providers (i.e. electricity, water, communications, etc.) located outside the "Organization". This is typically the rupture of supply (e.g. life line failure) resulting from an event occurring outside the "Organization" (e.g. explosion at the power plant, fire

at the national grid substation, collapse of Transmission and Distribution - T&D - lines).
Note that in some markets SI (utilities) are considered as suppliers and included in the CBI above.

Other BI Extension – Contingency extension: refers to any interruption of business suffered by the "Organization" caused by an event occurring outside the "Organization" and is different to the SI and CBI/CTE cases above. The event may be a decision taken by the authorities.
Note: as a rule of thumb the creativity of the (Re)Insurance industry should never be underestimated. Everything might be possible. So, any Contingency Extension may cover the gap or even, complete, extend, exceed or contradict an existing cover described above.

3.3. Note on "Contingency"

The word "Contingency" may introduce even more confusion.

The first definition is dated 1561: "A possible event, dependent on uncertainty, likely to happen to or as a result of something". This means, depending on the context:

- "An event likely to happen or to result in something"
- "An event likely to happen or as a result of something"

© Franck Orset (FPO)

Modern definition in Cambridge dictionary : "something that might possibly happen in the future, usually causing problems or making further arrangements necessary".

The A Inc case definitely fits the definition given above for CBI:

- An earthquake struck an island in eastern Asia in 1999, disabling a substation that provided electric power to two factories. Lacking power, the factories could not manufacture products they were supplying to a subsidiary of A Inc.

- When production resumed two weeks later, A Inc shipped orders from the island in eastern Asia via airfreight to meet its customers' needs for the Christmas season in North America, resulting in additional costs of more than USD 600 k.

- A Inc filed a claim for this loss under the "Contingent Time Element" provision of the all-risk manuscript property insurance policy issued to A Inc by North American Guarantee and Liability Insurance Company. North American Guarantee denied coverage, and A Inc filed a lawsuit on the grounds of lack of diversity.

- The following statement was reported during the trial: "Contingency is a misnomer; it simply means that the Insured's business interruption loss resulted from damage to a third-party's property".

4. BUSINESS INTERRUPTION (BI) FOCUS

4.1. BI Insurance

Business Interruption insurance is often misunderstood partly because of:

- The "**fear of the unknown**": Business interruption insurance is insurance cover that replaces business income lost in a "disaster". The term "disaster" in insurance language is replaced by "event" triggering the BI cover (the trigger). There is, of course, a time element underlying this definition. The duration of the interruption is the key factor to be investigated and to be clearly defined for a given occupancy in order to provide the adequate BI insurance cover. Unfortunately, most people have problems when it comes to imagining the worst case scenario occurring during very adverse conditions.

    People need to accept some facts first:
    - The worst doesn't just happen to other people.
    - A so-called "remote" event (having a very low probability) can happen tomorrow.
    - A single point of failure can compromise the entire "Organization".
    - After a major loss at their property they would not be able to restart their business for months, a year or two and, in some cases, even longer.

- **It differs throughout the world**: acronyms and terminologies are understood and used differently around the world depending on different factors such as culture, local markets and regulations, background, etc. Things are not always straightforward. BI is not a finite topic. There is no "approved" standardized definition or wording for BI cover. However, there are some commonly used forms and wording.

For example, in a Latin American market Business Interruption (BI) is called:
- o "Consequential Loss" further to a property loss (i.e. major fire in a plant).
- o "Loss of Profit" further to Machinery Breakdown (MB).

Best recommendations:
- o Think global and Act local", make sense of each case.
- o Trying hard to understand who is right or wrong would be a waste of time.
- o Better try to understand the meaning and look for a correspondence in your own language.
- o Just accept the differences if any. It will make you even more knowledgeable on the subject.

4.2. BI Effective Downtime

BI losses have traditionally been estimated by trying to determine how long it would take to repair whatever degree of damage a property sustained. It was therefore assumed that at low to moderate damage levels most businesses remain operational (no significant BI loss foreseen). This may result in a significant underestimation of the BI loss since building damage alone cannot explain total BI losses.

The BI Effective downtime can be defined as the number of days (months) it takes before a business can return to full operations following a catastrophic event and this is the central variable in estimating BI losses.

The causes of downtime fall into two categories:
- **Direct BI**: physical damage to an insured structure that causes a suspension of business activities and loss of business income because of the suspension.
- **Indirect BI**: can result from a wide range of circumstances such as lack of egress / ingress (e.g. flood), restricted access due to potential contamination or instability of the structure (i.e. further earthquake shock), police investigation (i.e. trying to define responsibilities), curfew (i.e. civil unrest after natural peril impact) or major impairment on utilities (i.e. power line down).

The key variable of the downtime can be divided into three successive phases:

- **Pre-Repair/Relocation**: time it takes to assess damage, obtain building permits, find and hire contractors (could be complicated in case of natural peril impacting an extended area. This would result in a lack of manpower). Some businesses may choose to relocate the property to a better place less exposed to natural perils (e.g. flood) or neighbors (e.g. a refinery from where the blast originated). In such cases available terrain must be found, authorizations must be granted, deals must be done.
- **Repair and Reconstruction/ Relocation**: Critical machinery and equipment having a relatively long lead time (e.g. 18 months for a transformer) may not be available. Construction material may have to be imported (e.g. Caribbean island impacted by a hurricane).
- **Post-Repair/Relocation**: after repairs are completed, business income will probably not immediately resume at the same level as before the event. It may take a very long time to regain the earlier market share. Experienced staff may be difficult to find. Certification of process lines (e.g. food, pharmaceutics) and quality certification (e.g. ISO) may take some months.

Each and every business is specific, so the three phases above will include different contingencies impacting their duration.

The total equivalent Business Interruption downtime is the sum of the duration all three successive phases above.

Business insurance may only partially cover this equivalent BI downtime. Some contingencies such as the loss of market share or loss of reputation are definitely not covered.

4.3. BI Financial Structure

Business Interruption can be defined financially or in accordance to a prescribed chart of accounts or taxonomy of accounts.

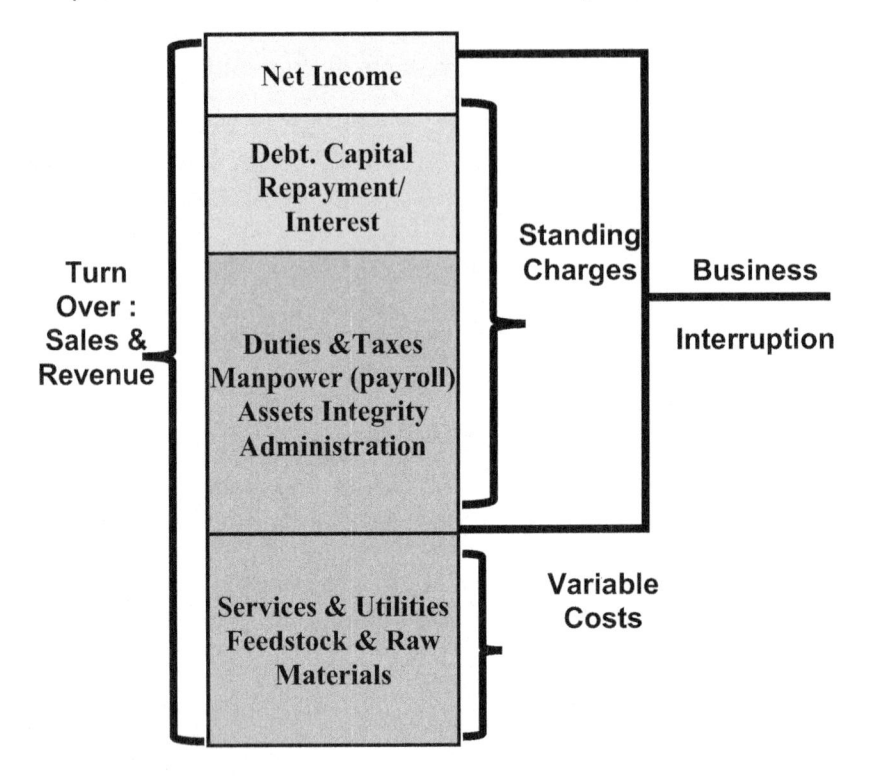

```
                    ┌─────────────────────────┐
                    │       Net Income        │
                    ├─────────────────────────┤
                    │    Debt. Capital        │
                    │    Repayment/           │
                    │    Interest             │   Standing
       Turn         ├─────────────────────────┤   Charges       Business
       Over:        │                         │
       Sales &      │    Duties & Taxes       │                 Interruption
       Revenue      │    Manpower (payroll)   │
                    │    Assets Integrity     │
                    │    Administration       │
                    ├─────────────────────────┤
                    │                         │
                    │    Services & Utilities │   Variable
                    │    Feedstock & Raw      │   Costs
                    │    Materials            │
                    └─────────────────────────┘
```

© Didier Schütz (DLS)

Almost each and every "Organization" has its own way of presenting BI. This is not, however, necessarily destined for Risk Management purposes nor for (Re)Insurance purposes.

Gross profit refers to the money a company earns after subtracting the costs associated with producing and selling its products. In accordance with the diagram above, the BI can be defined in different ways:

    BI = Gross profit - COGS (Cost Of Goods Sold)
       Net sales – Variable Costs
       Turn Over – Variable Costs
       Net Income + Standing Charges

When dealing with risk engineering and loss estimates, the most important thing is not to get confused by a definition or BI structure. Depending on your financial skill, the most affordable / comprehensive definition may be:

BI = Profit + Fixed Costs

Fixed costs: Operating expenses and other costs still being incurred by the property (based on historical costs).

4.4. BI as per Business Type

When speaking about BI from a loss estimate standpoint for (Re)Insurance purposes some people may have difficulties or prove to be reluctant because of the competitive aspect of figuring out where they actually make money and generate profit.

The BI structure may be surprisingly obvious for some high tech occupancies or even heavy industries involving very sophisticated processes.
Just follow the process stream to identify where and how the added value is generated at each and every step of the process.
Look for bottlenecks and single points of failure such as a unique piece of equipment or utility.

Some other occupancies such as hotels, not necessarily known for any particularly advanced process, may have a very complicated BI structure due to the way they are making money while fitting into a network of business partners.

For example, a hotel room may be sold as a stand-alone product for a certain time or can be part of a package including air transfer, ground transportation, cruises, tourism tours, sports activities, spa & health care, events such as weddings, corporate seminars, etc. Prices depend on demand and offer resulting in significant variations for the final client (as far as the final client / guest is concerned a hotel is largely like a plane where almost all passengers pay a different price.)

The "products" themselves may be sold through various channels including but not limited to hotel reservation systems, affiliated agents, travel agencies, internet, etc. At the end of the day all business partners will receive compensation.

Moreover, some hotels may have a gift shop and offer various services such as laundry, food, entertainment (e.g. a pool party with a famous DJ or a magic show), etc. This generates additional revenues. Additional and occasional manpower may be hired for special events or and during peak season.

The BI is directly dependent on the occupation rate.

This would make the BI structure and even the terminology in use somewhat complicated.

Example: a Resort & SPA BI calculation details as indicated by the Risk Manager on site:

Gross Package Revenue: (budget for 80-85% full occupation rate)	**1,000 million**
Less Travel Agent Fees:	(-20%)
Less Representative fees – Unique services:	(-8%)
Less 40% of Variable payroll:	(-5%)
Less Various Servicing, Food, Electricity, etc. Plus, other income, gift shops, laundry, etc.	(-8%) +3%
Sub Total:	62%
Plus Add back Unique Fees (purchase center):	+8%
BI: Total Financial Loss of Gross Package Revenue:	**70%**

4.4.1. Nominal BI

Some Organizations may speak about "Nominal BI" because of their very specific business. This is the case of a container harbor involved in maritime freight market.
For hundreds of years all cargo was loaded and unloaded in oddly sized wooden crates and barrels and in bulk. The process was very slow and laborious and certainly not standardized.

In the early 1950's in the US the owner of a trucking company began his own 'container concept' and had the first feasible concept and working system in 1956 with many patents. However, it was the US military which finally did what was necessary to create ISO.

Containers became accepted by every shipping line and every country of the world.

© Franck Orset (FPO)

Because containers were so much faster and organized to load-unload, the cost of loading freight was reduced by more than 90%.

Today, about 80% of all goods are shipped using intermodal shipping containers.
Intermodal means that marine cargo, truck, and rail networks are linked.

Containers may be transported by road to the harbor for shipping.

Containers may also be unloaded from a cargo ship prior to being loaded on a truck or on-loaded to another ship The Key Performance Indicator of a container harbor is the transit duration (service level).

For a given container or a group of containers this transit duration should be as short as possible.

Due to the high level of load handling complexity, containers are not always located per shipment in the same area. Modern containers include locator systems for each and every container in the harbor using geo-coordinates and raw levels and automated load handling vehicles.

In order to be profitable, the number of containers handled in a harbor should be the highest as possible (activity level). However, this can only be up to a certain point in order to prevent the harbor being totally saturated, slowing down loading / unloading operations which would result in a counterproductive situation with a very long transit duration.

This scissors effect is the same obtained with a filing cabinet in an office: too many files tightly packed in the cabinet would improve storage but prevent any easy access to files making this cabinet useless.

For some container harbors the nominal BI is defined by the number of containers (activity level) corresponding to 50 to 80% of the harbor yard capacity allowing for the shortest transit duration.

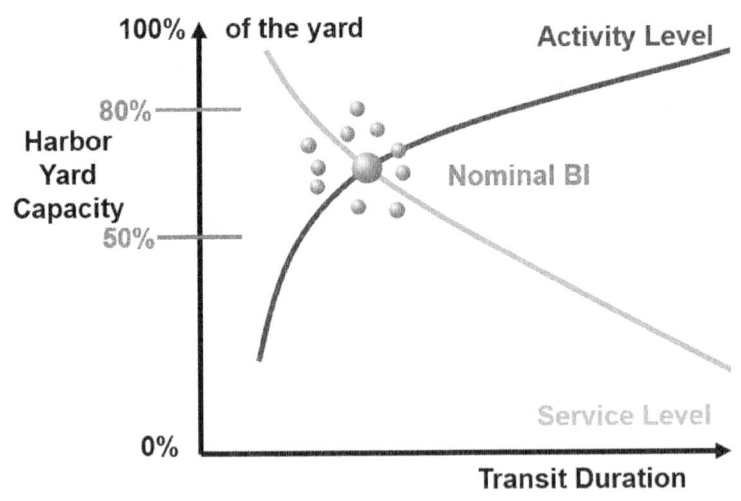

© Didier Schütz (DLS)

Based on the above, in case of loss at the container harbor, the BI should not be calculated on the maximum containers that could be kept in the harbor at a certain time but rather calculated considering the nominal number of containers corresponding to the nominal transit duration.

4.4.2. Delay in Start Up (DSU) / Advanced Loss Of Profit (ALOP)

Delay in Start Up (DSU) is also referred to as Advanced Loss of Profits (ALOP.

DSU / ALOP is used exclusively for engineering risks covered by a CAR / EAR policy.

CAR stands for Contractors' All Risks Insurance. This insurance provides cover to the contractors and their related works, equipment and third parties during the period of insurance. Due to the nature of work the period may be relatively long (e.g. 5 years).

EAR stands for the insurance coverage that covers the machinery whilst under installation.

DSU / ALOP can be assimilated to BI insurance for property. However, the following main specific points (amongst others) should be considered:

- A CAR/EAR project is where money is invested in anticipation of future returns.
- The DSU / ALOP Insurance covers the owner for the risk of losing profit. It is called 'Advanced' because the insurance is taken before business starts up. It is taken during the project implementation, before a plant is commissioned.

The larger the project, the larger the potential loss.
The longer the period, the higher the probability of an event occurring.
ALOP insurance therefore needs to be well designed for both parties involved (i.e. Insured, (Re)Insurers).

For example, designing an DSU / ALOP cover for the Basílica de la Sagrada Família in Barcelona would have been a challenge:

On 19 March 1882, construction of the Sagrada Família began under the architect Francisco de Paula del Villar. In 1883, when Villar resigned, Gaudí took over as chief architect, transforming the project with his architectural and engineering style, combining

Gothic and curvilinear Art Nouveau forms. Gaudí devoted the remainder of his life to the project, and he is buried in the crypt. At the time of his death in 1926, less than a quarter of the project was complete

Relying solely on private donations, the Sagrada Família's construction progressed slowly and was interrupted by the Spanish Civil War. In July 1936, revolutionaries set fire to the crypt and broke their way into the workshop, partially destroying Gaudí's original plans, drawings and plaster models, which led to 16 years of work to piece together the fragments of the master model. Construction resumed intermittently in the 1950s.

Advancements in technologies such as computer aided design and computerized numerical control (CNC) have since enabled faster progress and construction passed the midpoint in 2010.

It is anticipated that the building may be completed by 2026, the centenary of Gaudí's death.

4.5. BI Trends

As a matter of fact since the 1980's overall BI is gradually increasing for the majority of occupancies.

The part of BI compared to PD within Property insurance is growing. In the case of a major loss within the industry involving a critical piece of machinery, Property Damage would, in some cases, only represent 10% of the loss or even less.

Different factors can explain this prevailing BI such as those described in section 1.3 (The "ZOOG" Cocktail of which:
- Concentration of values and investments (in one site as opposed to two or three previously).
- Optimization of industrial flows (one plant is dedicated to one production + just-in-time production).
- Automation (increase of production rate).
- Use of new technologies (high-tech, sensitive equipment, specialized repair / calibration, long delivery time).

The following changes should also be considered for modern Organizations:

- Limited production investment for short term – middle term profitability: time being money, long term returns are usually no longer affordable except for state-owned operations aiming to develop the industry sector of a country (i.e. mineral sector).
- Switching from production to brainware (R&D) & distribution: all production tools and properties are relocated in cheaper (labor, taxes) countries. The remaining properties of the Organization located in the original country are dedicated exclusively to the design of the products, sending out orders to the production units, reception and distribution of Finished Products within huge Distribution Centers. The only machinery and equipment owned by the Organization being basically forklifts and cutters for respectively handling and opening the boxes!
- Production risk transfer and sub-contracted activities: production properties and tools are literally transferred to third parties producing on order for brainware (R&D) & distribution Organizations which are therefore 'service-oriented' (BI represents up to 80% and more) rather than 'production-oriented'.

Example 1: service-oriented companies:

- The W company located in Western Europe has specialized in the manufacturing of metal screws since 1945 and is comprised of several plants in one country.
- Over decades, the company has developed a wide range of products (e.g. mechanical fasteners and dedicated related tools for the customers).
- Today the W company is only involved in the design and distribution of the product. The production itself is subcontracted to Asian suppliers working on order for the company. Finished products are received by the W company Distribution Center in big cardboard boxes in containers. Cardboard boxes are opened, Finished Products are re-packaged, sold on e-shop or delivered to retailers or directly to customers (mostly professional) based on their consumption

which is monitored by the W company. The real added value here is the service in terms of supply management that is much appreciated by the customers.

Example 2: a loss involving a K company designing and selling ready-to-assemble furniture, kitchen appliances and home accessories, among other useful goods and occasionally home services:

- The retail shop comprises a multiple storey show room for the customers and a storage and pick up area including racks in a high bay warehouse.
- A fire broke out during an idle period in a retail shop. The retail shop was totally lost.
- The building was rented to a British investor (PD: about USD 15Miuo) also impacted by a loss of rent after the loss.
- For the K company the loss was basically Business Interruption:
    - Property Damage: additions and improvement to building USD 1 million.
    - Business Interruption: around USD 25 million based on annual turnover.

Example 3: a rail tunnel for shuttle for trucks and trailers:
- Fire on a freight shuttle resulting in a total loss of the shuttle (rolling stock) and damage to the structure of the tunnel (reinforced concrete). No passengers injured (truck drivers grouped in the amenity railcar located behind the locomotive): 8 months needed for the reinstatement of the damaged section of the tunnel. In the mean-time the tunnel was operating at 50% of its full capacity using crossovers. This led to a bill of:
    - PD&BI: € 280 million of which:
    € 40 million Rolling Stock
    € 50 million Tunnel repair
    BI: € 190 million

Example 4: a loss within an Organization with a high level of Industrial flow optimization:

- The Organization produces active components and intermediate products for pest control (fungicides, herbicides and insecticides) at its site in Western Europe. The site includes several buildings of which some are made of a steel frame design with an infill of brickwork. The production-related equipment includes boilers, distillation machines, vessels, centrifuges, vaporizers, mixers, pumps and pipes necessary for the production flow.

- A fire broke out during the filling process in a building while an employee was feeding the unit with the chemical product Hexothiozine. Approximately 4,000 kg Hexothiozine combusted. The area directly affected by the fire was a surface of roughly 80 m². Further spreading of the fire was avoided by the immediate action of the plant fire brigade.

- Subject to a final assessment by a structural engineer, the building (steel frame design with an infill of brickwork) itself seems not to have sustained any material damage.

- The acid-resistant floor has to be replaced, two window facades and the light roof are to be renewed, cleaning-up works are to be executed. Costs-in so far are expected to be roughly around € 1 million.

- Various devices have been destroyed or at least damaged by fire and heat. Examination as to whether the equipment might be repaired or must be replaced has not yet finished. The damage of the equipment is assessed, at first glance, to be roughly around € 6 million.

- The fire damage interrupted the production of HTC for at least 3 months. HTC is an active component used for the protection of seeds against pest infestation and sold either in its pure form or as an ingredient of combined products. According to a first approximate calculation of the loss handling committee (which is composed of representatives of the Insured, the Insured's captive and various loss adjusters) the Insured is expected to lose a production amount of 600 t.

- Efforts to bridge the BI loss (BI mitigation) are nearly impossible due to:

- o No stock: an excellent market situation! The insured has no material stock reserves available.
- o Single site: the affected production site is the only one the insured has for the production of HTC.
- o No alternative supplier / no spare capacity: an acquisition of HTC on the market is not possible as the insured's worldwide single competitor does not have any free capacity.
- Overall, the gross loss of revenue might total € 130 million of which:
  - o Direct BI: This might mean a loss of turnover of € 95 with a corresponding loss of profit contribution of € 80 million.
  - o Induced BI:

    Interruption of the production process of the component UMD for two days with a shortfall of 40t and a profit contribution loss of € 4 million.

    Further side effects of the fire damage to other production areas might cause an additional BI loss of € 15 million.
- Loss of market share expected:
  - o Adverse effects on the production of hydrofluoric acid and the reluctance of clients to purchase products which are typically bought together with HTC-products (leader product).
  - o The loss amount is uncertain (between € 10 million and loss of profit contribution Induced BI on initiated new Business of € 80 million may be expected depending on parties involved).
- So called BI loss on initiated New Business:
  - o Furthermore, the insured had concretely planned to expand its HTC production. This project had already been approved by the board and budgeted. The main reason for this planned extension of production was the fact that the Insured had won a new large customer.
  - o Although the relevant contract with this customer has not yet been signed the Insured asserts that negotiations are

very close to a successful ending and that the effect on this new business relation is part of the Insured's business plan for 2013 and the following years.
- o The fire damage will mean a substantial delay of the delivery process and might provoke entirely new negotiations, the impact of which is currently difficult to evaluate but could amount to an additional loss of € 45 million should things develop unfavorably.
- Based on the above the PD & BI loss reported by the Insured would be around € 262 million of which only € 6 million PD and € 1 million for cleaning and € 255 million for the loss of revenue.

4.6. BI Volatility

"The line between gambling and investing is artificial and thin. The soundest investment has the defining trait of a bet (you losing all of your money in hopes of making a bit more), and the wildest speculation has the salient characteristic of an investment (you might get your money back with interest)."
— Michael Lewis, The Big Short: Inside the Doomsday Machine

Speculative commodities may have a significant impact on the income of a company (profit) and therefore on its Business Interruption depending on the market conditions (current offer and demand) and stock exchange situation (speculation on commodity availability).

Speculative commodities are numerous. As far as BI is concerned these commodities can be divided in two main groups and the list is not exhaustive:

Raw Material or Feedstock	Finished or Processed Products
Oil	Hydrocarbons
Gold, palladium, silver	Agricultural, fertilizers
Diamonds	Refined products (paper pulp)
Natural gas	Alumina
Iron, phosphate ore	Silicon
Etc.	Etc.

Due to the high volatility of some commodities, the benefit can be much higher or lower than the annual plan. The declared BI insurance value can appear either over-evaluated or under-evaluated when a loss occurs resulting in interruption of the production. A certain variation (plus and minus) is therefore admitted in some insurance cover and the BI figures need to be reviewed regularly.

4.7. BI as per Insurance Wording

Important notice about BI Insurance – This is NOT:
- a "Nice to have cover"
- a "One size fits all"

BI Insurance should be tailored to the exposure, factoring in the occupancy and related hazards, the surrounding exposures and natural perils of the area where the Organization is located.

Let's focus on the most common case consisting of BI being included as part of the business' primary policy (Property cover). It only pays out if the cause of the loss is covered by the overarching policy.

It is very important to identify the underlying cover which triggers BI. The following chain rule should apply for a BI cover to be triggered:
1. Physical Damage (PD) or Loss
2. To the insured property
3. Of the type covered as per the insurance policy
4. Which causes an interruption
5. For a defined Indemnity period

Example 1:
- A plastic toy manufacturing plant is fully destroyed by a fire.
- Re-instatement period (debris removal, building to be rebuilt, new machinery and equipment to be manufactured, shipped, installed, tested) is estimated at 12 months.

- The plant is insured for PD and BI as an extension of the Property Cover (12 months indemnity period: benefit + fixed costs) on the basis of a named perils policy called "FLEXA" (Fire, Lightning, Explosion, Aircraft).
- The named perils of the property Policy are also called "governing perils".
- In such a case both PD and BI covers are triggered in accordance with the chain rule above.

Example 2:
- A metal workshop is flooded due to the nearest river overflowing following heavy rain.
- The re-instatement period (waiting for the end of the flood, attempt to clean some electric driven machinery and equipment by a specialized company, replacement of certain tools) is estimated at 5 months.
- The plant is insured for PD and BI as an extension of the Property Cover (12 months indemnity period: benefit + fixed cost) on the basis of an All Risk policy except for earthquake, flood, windstorm and cyber attack.
- Flood being excluded, the Property cover won't be triggered
- Because the Property cover has not been triggered the BI covers won't be triggered either in accordance with the chain rule above.

Note that in some very few cases BI may be part of a standalone policy in certain jurisdictions. These covers only pay out if the cause of the loss is a defined event. These standalone policies are not as common as the general case described above.

4.7.1. BI Components

Note that some insureds may choose to declare the BI on fixed costs only but not on the profits, or on a mix of both depending on the investment type. Example, for a major group owning several properties around the world:
- Own properties called Own Direct Investment (ODIs): BI cover for fixed costs only.

- Joint venture operations: BI cover for fixed costs + profits

4.7.2. Main types of BI cover

There are basically two main types of insurance cover:
- Gross Earnings basis (so-called American Cover).
- Gross Profit basis (so-called English Cover).

The scope of coverage and the key parameters are summarized in the following table:

BI Cover Type	Gross Earnings (so-called US form)	Gross Profit (so-called UK form)
Scope of coverage	So called "American / US Form of BI Cover" # Business Income insurance to cover the losses suffered by the business during the period of restoration of the property after the loss. Coverage range: "Directly caused by…" Finished goods loss excluded. Increase costs: Extra Expense.	So called "British / UK Form of BI Cover" # Business Interruption insurance (Additions or Difference basis) to regain the "financial" position they would have been in had an insurable event not occurred. Coverage range: "In consequence of…" Finished goods loss included Increase costs: ICOW
Indemnity Period	Based on interruption period – time to repair or replace No pre-determined maximum indemnity period(*)	Based on Maximum Indemnity Period selection. Pre-determined maximum indemnity period (limited)
Loss amount covered	Net Profit + Fixed Charges	12 month turnover before event + adjustment for special circumstances and business trends

(*) Having no pre-determined maximum indemnity period with the Gross Earnings cover (so called American Cover) is not surprising especially when it concerns a business on a very competitive market such as in the US. It would be nonsensical to delay the reinstatement of the business. This would lead to the loss of market share and customers being tempted away by other suppliers taking advantage of this interruption. The market share would eventually be lost forever should the reinstatement take too long. BI cover in this case would provide just enough cash flow for the organization to survive prior to resuming business.

In real life / the real world the situation is not quite so cut and dry. The world is not split between these two types of cover. The most common resulting cover looks like a Gross Earnings cover (American Cover) with a pre-determined maximum indemnity period (e.g. usually 12, 18 up to 24, 36, 48 months in some cases depending on occupancy in class and related exposures).

Having a pre-determined maximum indemnity period is very important for the (Re)Insurer. The reinstatement period may be very long in some cases due to adverse conditions which, more often than not, cannot be predicted.

For example:

- A cement factory established in Asia in the 1980's was badly destroyed by a tsunami in 2004.
- The owner had to invest USD 90 million to rebuild the factory of which 85 was paid out by the insurance market as part of the Property cover.
- The factory was expected to return to business in mid-2007.
- Due to adverse conditions including access issues (infrastructures being severely damaged), administrative difficulties, lack of labor force (various villages destroyed, a lot of people dead and missing) etc., the plant only got back to business at the end of 2010.

4.7.3. Other costs that may be associated to BI:

- **Extra expenses**: reimbursement for reasonable expenses (other than fixed costs) that allow the business to continue operations while the property is being repaired.
- **Temporary location**: some policies cover the extra expenses of moving to, and operating from, a temporary location.
- **Commission and training costs**: Business Interruption (BI) policies essentially cover the cost of providing training to the operators of machinery replaced by the insurer following the insured events.

4.8. Sub-Product BI or Derivate BI

4.8.1. Cogeneration

Some plants may generate waste heat from their process that may be recovered through heat exchangers or economizers used for producing steam. The steam can then be used to run a Steam Turbine Generator producing electric power.

The steam can be used for the process itself (i.e. steam heated and/or run machinery) or it can be sold to the nearest plant for their process (e.g. the dryers of a saw mill).

The electric power issued from cogeneration can be used by the plant itself in order to reduce the cost of production and its dependence on the national grid. The surplus power can be sold to the grid. Some countries that lack public electric power generation capacity tend to encourage the production of electric power from industries via incentives and very attractive prices. In some other countries, there is only an agreement with the grid for exporting electric power on a seasonal basis (no profit for the plant).

The market conditions for some commodities are so competitive that the margins are very low. This is the case of such mass products as sugar but also bio-fuel. In some cases, the revenue made on electric power generation is relatively substantial. Some facilities may even increase their electric power production capacity through the installation of modern power generators representing large values in term of property. In some cases, this may change the class of occupancy of the plant switching it from an agricultural commodity producer to an energy service provider.

For example: a sugar mill producing raw and refined sugar from sugarcane and ethanol / hydrated ethanol from fermented sugar in a distillery. Sugar is sold on the market when the price is economically suitable or stored on-site waiting for better market conditions. The ethanol is sold to famous brands of rum and to the state as bio-fuel for the automotive business. The bagasse is the dry pulpy fibrous residue that remains after sugarcane or sorghum stalks are crushed to extract their juice. It is used as biofuel for the production of heat through a boiler producing steam. The high pressure steam is used to run 12 Steam Turbine Generators that produce electricity (total installed capacity of 300MW) used at the plant but it is also sold to the grid. The low pressure steam is used in the process of water evaporation in the sugar mill and as a heating media for the distillation process. The total revenue made though electric power generation represents about 25% of the total BI and 200% of the revenue made by the distillery.

For some integrated installations, steam and electricity used for internal feed and consumption purposes may result in a very complicated billing process. SUPPLY OF SERVICES AND UTILITIES AGREEMENTS may exist between the different process units and also with the national grid when electric power is sold and/or purchased depending on the needs. The steam may be sold internally or externally, and the price may be calculated as an equivalent of electricity produced that may be sold or purchased from the grid. Moreover, electric power may be purchased from the grid at a high price while electric power is sold to the grid at a low price. Electric power may also be exported to the grid to run a reverse osmosis plant producing fresh water for the nearest community. In such cases, the total BI resulting from the loss of one Steam Boiler and /or one Steam Turbine Generator unit on the installation may have a big impact and the resulting BI may be very difficult to predict.

4.8.2. Carbon Credit

Carbon credit is issued from the carbon credit system which was ratified in conjunction with the 1995 Kyoto Protocol. Its goal is to stop the increase of carbon dioxide emissions. The carbon credit system looks to reduce emissions by having countries honoring their emission quotas and offers incentives for being below them.

Credits are awarded to countries or groups that have reduced their greenhouse gases below their emission quota. This is a permit that allows the holder to emit one ton of carbon dioxide. Carbon credits can be traded on the international market at their current market price.

For example, if an environmental group plants enough trees to reduce emissions by one ton, the group will be awarded a credit.

If a steel producer has an emissions quota of 10 tons, but is expecting to produce 11 tons, it could purchase this carbon credit from the environmental group. This is considered as revenue for the environmental group.

The price of carbon credits is calculated by a financial instrument called CER (- linked) Bonds or "Coupon Equivalent Rate". Carbon Credit can be also named as per these financial instruments on the declared Total Sum Insured spread sheet. This may sometimes give rise to some confusion. But again, don't be fooled by these business buzz words.

As a summary, a carbon credit is a generic term for any tradable certificate or permit representing the right to emit one ton of carbon dioxide or the equivalent amount of a different greenhouse gas (tCO2e).

Carbon credit is therefore considered as revenue for the group being awarded a credit. This, then, affects BI.

There is much criticism of this Carbon credit trade (e.g. "pollution permit designed to be profitable").

Let's consider a modern plant such as a pulp mill equipped with all the state of the art gas and dust emission control systems allowing production of cellulosic pulp from eucalyptus trees from the nearest forest. The emission of greenhouse gases at full production capacity is below its emission quota for such an occupancy in its class. Every year the pulp mill is awarded a credit which is sold on the market. This is part of the pulp mill's revenue as is the surplus electric power generated from the heat and steam of the process which is sold to the grid. This pulp mill is insured for Property Damage but also for a "triple column BI" including pulp production, electric power generation and carbon credit. In case of a major event of the type covered in the Property policy resulting in a physical loss at the pulp mill and a process shut down for a certain period of time the BI cover will be triggered for the 3 types of revenue. It may appear a little bit strange for a carbon credit to be compensated for by (Re)Insurance and paid out to a non-operating plant. However, this is considered as revenue and should be considered as such for BI assessment and loss Estimates as explained below.

4.9. BI Assessment

BI assessment should be done in accordance with the intended use. BI calculated for Risk Management purposes may differ from the BI calculated for tax reporting or financial use.

Let's focus exclusively on BI assessment from a Risk Management perspective, thus including Risk Financing such as (Re)Insurance. The intention is to identify and assess the event that generates the largest loss in monetary terms including Property Damage and Business Interruption loss amounts and period durations.

The process flow and physical location of production lines should be well understood. Here are some of the things that must be taken into account:

- Define process type.
- Raw Materials (internal external suppliers / back up / buffer storage on-site / off-site).

- Packaging (internal external suppliers / back up / buffer storage on-site / off-site).
- Number of lines / Location / Layout.
- Redundancies / Bottlenecks.
- Critical Machinery & Equipment.
- Finished Products (customers, loading facilities, shipment, transportation).
- Critical Utilities (steam, water, electricity, cooling).
- Environmental considerations (regulations).

The simplest way of doing this assessment is usually a "what-if" analysis or study. This consists of plugging in different scenarios and values to determine a range of possible outcomes. This type of analysis is often done when data is limited, and an Organization wants to make the most informed decision possible.

For such an analysis, all potential scenarios should be clearly identified. All special hazards and events (man-made, internal and external including surrounding exposures, natural perils) that may impact a given Organization should be listed.

Warning:
- Considering probabilities for a given event at this stage but neglecting a scenario deemed as remote as per low probability but that may occur tomorrow (as allowed by probabilities) is dangerous.
- Overestimating the Emergency Plan (i.e. early detection, fire fighters, salvage operations) in such a way that 'the worst can only ever happen to someone else' may be completely wrong.
- Considering mitigating factors such as a potential Contingency Plan and Business Continuity Plan may lead to a very optimistic portrayal of the situation whereas, in real life, a loss may occur under the worst adverse conditions possible (don't forget Murphy's law).
- Considering each and every facility of a plant or a complex as fully independent may result in underestimating the impact of

an event on the whole chain of production. The relationship between the different facilities should be considered.
- The above consideration also extends to sister plants of the same organization that have a business link (i.e. two sister plants A and B being the two-step process of a product, Plant B processing the semi-finished products produced at plant A. See interdependencies section).

For example, a factory producing cookies:
- This factory comprises a certain level of vertical integration producing its own flour from wheat grain through a milling unit and the final packaging (cardboard boxes) for the cookies.
- Steam for the process is produced on site by the cardboard plant (steam-heated process).
- The effluent from the cardboard plant, using a large amount of water, is treated by the innovative effluent treatment plant using worms prior to being released into the sewer network as required by local regulations. Without this effluent treatment the cardboard plant could not operate.
- The Total Sum Insured given by the financial and insurance department shows the following:

Process Unit	Building	Content / M&E	PD $Mio	BI (12 months) $Mio	Indemnity Period (months)	BI ($Mio)	PB&BI $Mio
Mill wheat (silos & milling)	20	40	60	20	20	33	93
Sub Total Fire Area 1:	20	40	60	20		33	93
Central Utilities	5	35	40	5	24	10	50
Admin building, canteen	6	2	8	0		0	8
Workshops & Offices	2	1	3	0		0	3
Site Fire Water Supply	0,2	0,8	1	0		0	1
Total Fire Area 2:	13	39	52	5		10	62
Cookie factory	50	80	130	150	22	275	405
Cardboard plant	10	30	40	20	22	37	77
Sub Total Fire Area 3:	60	110	170	170		312	482
Distribution Center	80	10	90	0		0	90
Sub Total Fire Area 4:	80	10	90	0		0	90
Effluent treatment plant	1	1	2	0		0	2
Sub Total Fire Area 5:	1	1	2	0		0	2
Total:	174	200	374	195		355	729

M&E: Machinery & Equipment

Some remarks:
- The main facilities are grouped by fire areas separated by physical distances.
- Indemnity periods are based on the replacement / reinstatement time of a critical process being impacted by a major event (i.e. scenario based).
- The given BI shows different indemnity periods (20-22-24 months) based on the replacement time of the most critical machinery & equipment in these areas (i.e. 20 months for replacing the milling unit after a dust explosion, 24 months for replacing the steam boiler in case of explosion, 22 months for reinstating the cookie factory or the cardboard plant in case of fire).

The above assessment is somehow very promising, but it doesn't consider the business relationship between the different process units, utilities and storage area. One event impacting one of these areas will also have a direct impact on the others. The process flow should be considered. For example, a dust explosion at the mill would result in all downstream operations shutting down for 20 months. An explosion at the Central Utility may result in all upstream and downstream operations shutting down for 24 months. A major electric fire at the Effluent Treatment Plant will result in the shut-down (administrative closure) of the cardboard plant for at least 4 months (time needed for replacing electric cabinets). The loss of the Distribution Center may have an impact as well (not described).

For such a "what-if" analysis, all possible scenarios should be considered. This includes:
- A major loss such as an explosion or fire destroying an entire facility. This is the most common scenario for numerous industrial and commercial risks including commodities storage. Between 12 and 24 months BI expected. Natural perils scenarios may need to be investigated in exposed areas (e.g. tsunami, earthquake, windstorm, even hail for automotive manufacturing that have all Finished Products on the parking lot).

- Catastrophic failure of critical process equipment. This scenario is dedicated to some specific occupancies. Accurate assessment should be carried out by a specialist):
    - Cement plant: explosion of the rotary kiln due to incomplete combustion or no adequate safety combustion causing gas to accumulate. Total loss of the kiln including cyclone tower and auxiliaries. Up to 18-24 months BI expected.
    - Steel Mill: blast furnace, Electric Arc Furnace steam explosion due to water trapped in molten material or even High Pressure Rupture of vessel used for direct reduction. Up to 18-24 months BI expected.
    - Pulp & paper: explosion of the Black Liquor Recovery Boiler (BLRB). At least 18 months BI.
    - Wood processing complex in Latin America: one effluent treatment plant used for 5 wood-board plants using new technology. There is only one filter supplier located in Poland. The replacement cost is around USD 1M. This is done every year. Filter manufacturing takes at least 3 months and at least 1 month needed for shipment.
    - Fume treatment used for power generation units consisting of an electrostatic precipitator (ESP). Around 12 months replacement in case of explosion. In the meantime the power generation unit might have to shut down depending on environmental regulations.
    - Aluminum smelter: pot freeze (solidification of aluminum) due to power failure. Up to 18-24 months reinstatement.
    - Semiconductor Plant: major fire and contamination of the clean room. Up to 18 months BI.
    - Oil & Gas: escape of liquid pressurized gas and Vapor Cloud Explosion (VCE). 24 to 36 months BI and maybe even more.
    - Mining: machinery breakdown impacting a Semi-Autogenous Grinder (SAG-mill) handling part of the production. Repair may take several months including shipping overseas. From 8 to 24 months BI. Collapse of part of the open cast mine pit including the haul road. Up to 12 months BI and more. Major loss impacting the barrel or the hoist of an underground mine. Up to 12-24 month BI expected.

- Critical utility loss:
  - Electric substation, electric room, Motor Control Center: a major fire could lead to the entire loss of a substation / room. Depending on equipment, the reinstatement time could take a minimum of 4 months and up to 6 - 8 months in case of special equipment such as Variable Speed Controllers. Example: a 200km long slurry pipeline used to send the ore from the mine to the chemical processing site. The head station comprises a main electric room housing a variable speed controller for the slurry pumps. In the case of a major fire inside this room the Property Damage is estimated at around USD 20 million with a BI of 8 months for manufacturing and installing the variable speed controller cabinets representing a BI loss amount of USD 1 billion.
  - Power Generation Unit: Disintegration and subsequent fire of Steam Turbine Generators and Gas Turbine would lead to at least 18 - 24 months BI. The replacement of a rotor may take 18 months.
  - Depending on capacity and specification, the replacement of a power transformer, Rectifier Transformer or Electric Arc Furnace may take a minimum of 18 months.
  - Cooling tower: despite the relatively low cost (i.e. USD 200-600k average for medium size) the lead time may be at least 4 months. Cooling towers are usually wet when operating. These towers are dry during maintenance periods and may be easily ignited resulting in a total loss due to the high combustible load (wood, Polyvinyl Chloride, Fiber Reinforced Plastics). In the meantime, the related process unit may have to stop due to the lack of an alternative cooling source. Some effluent (e.g. pulp mill) may have to be cooled as per regulations prior to being released in the river in order to prevent a rise in the river temperature that would kill all wild life.
  - Air blowers, air compressors, Air Separation Plant, Reverse Osmosis Plant, Effluent Treatment Plant, Fume / Gas Treatment Center, Electrostatic Precipitators are usually critical to the process. In the case of a major loss impacting these units, a relatively long BI for the related unit may also be expected (e.g. 4-6-8, 12 months).

- Example: a 20m² room housing Constant Current Regulator cabinets in an airport for the lighting of the runway. Should fire break out in this room, the reinstatement would take at least 3 months. In the meantime, night flights would have to be cancelled. Thus, there would be a corresponding loss of revenue for the airport concession.

All aggravating factors should be considered:
- Difficult or even impossible access (e.g. flood, Earthquake): after the 2004 tsunami in some islands of Indonesia the bridges were destroyed and could not be rebuilt for months. About 9 months after the Thai flood event in 2011, some industrial sites were not accessible and were still partially flooded by water trapped in the retention areas.
- Investigation periods may take longer than expected if there have been casualties. Authorities may want to establish the liability for each and every party involved. Example: major fire and total loss of an industrial bakery in Belgium. The ignition of the building was due to a truck on fire under a non-protected canopy. The rest of the plant was made of sandwich panels with highly combustible insulation and protected with automatic sprinkler protection. The truck was 3 years old. The authorities conducted an investigation involving the plant, the truck supplier and the cooling unit manufacturer. This delayed the reconstruction of the site for 6 months.
- Constraints imposed by the authorities may include the principle of precaution should there be any suspicion of air, ground or water table contamination. Example: an industrial site storing gypsum by-products of the process on a 40m high stack over a wide area. A dewatering system was in place. A leakage of water was detected at the center of the stack resulting from a sinkhole. This was a well-known phenomenon in the region. However, it was considered an impossible eventuality. The risk was acid water from the gypsum contaminating the 100m aquifer layer. A lot of wells used by farmers in this area were sourced in this layer. In order to prevent any administrative closure of operations, the industrial site carried out 2 main actions: 1) they plugged the penetration of the aquifer level with cement. This required the installation of a concrete pad and cement preparation unit on site. 2) They

took thousands of samples from the farmers' wells over a 6 month period and communicated the results using all possible suitable media. The overall cost was about USD 60 million of which 50% was just for communication.
- Contamination. Smoke resulting from fire may contaminate very sensitive facilities and /or machinery and equipment (e.g. clean room, surgery rooms, server rooms). Cleaning may take a relatively long time. Some equipment may have to be sent back to the manufacturer located overseas for cleaning and recalibration, thus extending the BI period.
- Debris removal after a fire involving material classified as hazardous for humans such as Askarel known as PCBs (Poly Chlorinated Biphenyls) which were used as transformer oil before the 80's as they have a high dielectric strength and are not flammable. However, these oil and byproducts after combustion are known to be very toxic for humans (endocrine perturbator). Cleaning operations may be long and difficult requiring special Personal Protective Equipment and the installation of waste treatment facilities.

Example 1: a fire in a plant resulting in the collapse of a large part of the roof. The debris removal took 8 months longer than standard due to tiles made of cement containing asbestos fibers.

Example 2: a fire engulfed an old heritage building melting and vaporizing several tons of lead used at the time of the construction. Investigation, potential decontamination and precaution measures delayed the reconstruction operations initially planned for at least 5 years.
- Seasonality of production. A loss occurring during low season of production (if any) will have a smaller impact than a loss occurring during peak season. Example: a plastic processing plant producing food boxes in the US. The high season for the production is from January to May. The products are stored on-site at the end of the production line before being sent to retailers in June. Most of the sales take place during the summer time. It is better to consider the loss that would occur at the end of the high production season for calculating the BI (e.g. total loss of the stock to be sold).

- Certification: the production line of some products may have to be certified prior to commencing operations. This is the case of most pharmaceutical products (e.g. European Medicines Agency, Food & Drugs administration in the US), equipment for labs, hospital, aviation (e.g. Federal Aviation Agency in the US) and other quality insurance programs (e.g. ISO 9000, 14000 for environment) for other products. This may result in a longer BI period than initially expected.
- The lead time of equipment is usually underestimated. Actually, as a rule of thumb, just consider that there is "Nothing on the shelves". Orders for critical spares and machinery and equipment are usually on a waiting list (please refer to the "ZOOG" cocktail for the causes).
- Internal procurement policies may constitute an aggravating factor. Some publicly owned companies need to run a tender as per regulations (mandatory). Example: after a loss in an electrics room in a calcination unit at a mine site in North Africa, all electrical equipment had to be replaced including an electric cabinet with a delivery time of 7 months (assembled in France with special components from Asia). However, the loss adjustment process combined with the internal anti-bribery procurement process including a tender took a total of 25 months.

4.10. BI Loss Estimate

This is maybe the shortest and most straightforward section of the document. The best recommendation is just to be conservative.

In actual fact, BI represents the largest part of the loss amount in a major loss. Mitigation tends to be non-efficient because of the intrinsic weakness of the measures.

As a result of the above, when assessing BI for insurance purposes look for the main scenarios and also the worst case scenario:
- Do not consider any potential mitigation measure.
- Consider direct BI for the facility where the loss occurred.

- The effective downtime (see previous sections) should be used for BI Loss estimates. The estimate of this effective downtime should be based on the scenario(s) generating the largest loss(es) in monetary terms (combined Property Damage and Business Interruption).
- Note that when the effective downtime is unknown and a BI cover exists, the BI assessment for the (Re)Insurer should be at least equal to 100% of the BI loss amount over the entire indemnity period. In this case the BI loss estimate is only useful for the (Re)Insurer so that he can gain an idea of his exposure. However, the BI period may be much longer for the insured (see aggravating factors above) and may result in a situation of inadequate insurance. Example: an integrated steel mill is insured for Property and BI over an 18 month period. However, the BI loss estimate shows that the replacement of the Direct Reduction Reactor following a High Pressure Vessel explosion would actually be 24 months.
- Consider potential BI for other operations (sister plants) upstream and downstream that may be impacted by the facility where the loss is originating (see next section "Interdependencies").
- Some insureds may choose different indemnity covers for different process units within the same plant based on possible scenarios. Example: a pulp mill with a Black Liquor Recovery Boiler known for having a high steam explosion potential (18 months BI cover purchased for explosion) and the rest of the plant for just fire potential (12 months BI cover purchased for fire).

5. INTERDEPENDENCIES (INDUCED BI) FOCUS

5.1. Mutually Reliant on Each Other

Interdependence can be defined as business link(s) or Interaction or "Mutual Interference" between different production operations within a plant, and/or between locations within the Organization, company or corporation.

It is important to note that:

Interdependencies may not be apparent without an in-depth investigation (use the process flow chart).

Example: ACME(*) tomato sauce factory.

- The production is seasonal once a year during summer time processing all tomatoes from surrounding farmers. The Finished Product (tomato sauce in vacuum-sealed plastic bags in metal drums) is stored with up to 4 drums piled on top of each other on a paved yard inside the premises. It is stored for about 40 weeks (subject to a quarantine random inspection).
- The tomato sauce, as such, is considered to be a low added value Work In Progress product (or semi-finished) and needs to be re-processed in one of the other facilities of the group - ACME ketchup factory- to produce elaborate high value products.
- The tomato sauce factory is located in an earthquake exposed area. A strong shake occurred in 2010 (second most powerful earthquake never recorded). No major structural damages were reported to the buildings and equipment. However, several drums stored in the yard collapsed (domino effect) and some of those were damaged spilling the tomato sauce.
- This led to the loss of 50,000 tons of products (rejected) corresponding to USD 57 million of Property Damages and a 1 day Business Interruption at the tomato sauce factory.
- It also led to an induced BI corresponding to 9 months production (seasonal) at ACME Ketchup Factory because of the lack of Work In Progress material to be processed.

(*) ACME: "Amazing Company that Makes Everything"

Warning: in some countries "Interdependence" or "Induced BI" is called "Internal CBI". This is a misnomer that can lead to severe confusion.

In other countries (e.g. Brazil) Induced BI due to interdependences may have a dedicated and lower limit than the BI insurance.

From a (Re)Insurance standpoint the way Induced BI due to interdependences is declared for (Re)Insurance purposes can make a big difference in the case of a loss as detailed in the following sections.

5.2. Induced BI as Downstream BI accumulation

In the following case, Plant A is considered as the main bottleneck supplying Work In Progress material to Plant B and Plant C downstream. Plant B and Plant C are independent from an operational standpoint.

In the case of a major event impacting Plant A, the downstream sister Plants B and C will have to shut down resulting in induced BI.

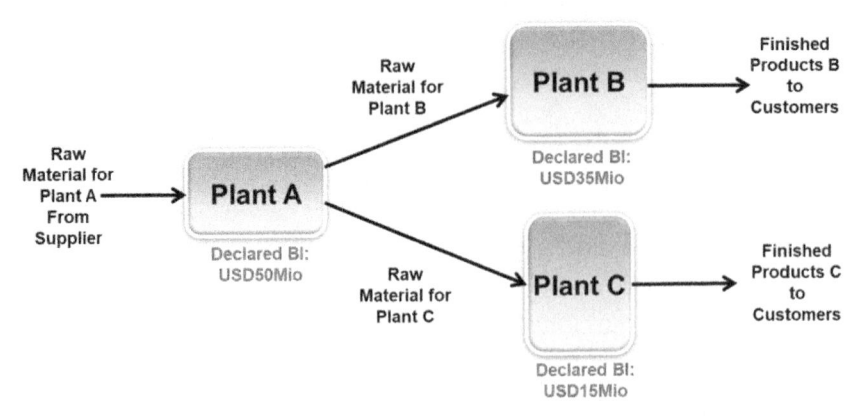

© Didier Schütz (DLS)

The declared BI for Plant A therefore corresponds to the sum of Plant B and Plant C.

From a BI perspective this is a valid point of view based on the process flow.

5.3. Induced BI as Upstream Extra Costs

Same example as above but "Extra Costs" declared instead of BI for Plant A.:

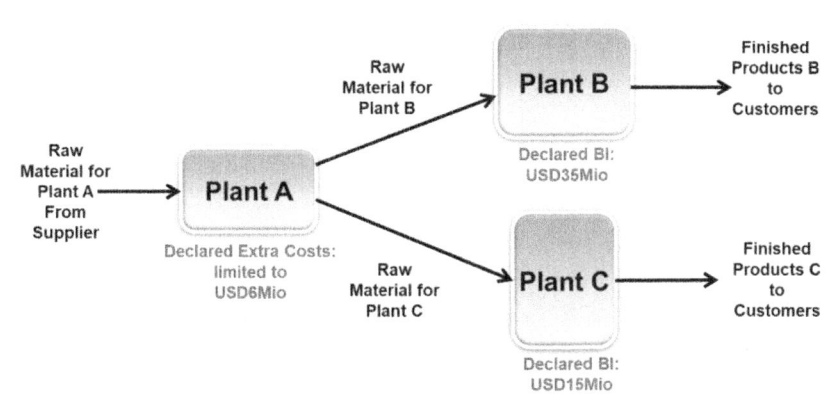

[Diagram: Raw Material for Plant A From Supplier → Plant A (Declared Extra Costs: limited to USD6Mio) → Raw Material for Plant B → Plant B (Declared BI: USD35Mio) → Finished Products B to Customers; Plant A → Raw Material for Plant C → Plant C (Declared BI: USD15Mio) → Finished Products C to Customers]

© Didier Schütz (DLS)

Consider that in the case of a major loss at Plant A, Raw Material for Plants B and C will be purchased on the market generating an extra cost of production.

This point of view is only valid if alternative supplier(s) is (are) already identified and contract(s) are signed. Otherwise, trying to find alternative supplies right after a major loss at Plant A would be virtually impossible. Several months may be needed.

5.4. Induced BI as Extra Costs per Event

In the following example there is no BI declared for any of the two Plants D and E.

In the case of a loss, Extra Costs are declared and are limited to USD 15 million <u>per plant</u> for purchasing Raw Materials / Finished Products on the market.

The goal, in the case of a major loss at Plant D, is to maintain the supply to the final customer (so as not to lose any market share) with Finished Products similar to those normally delivered from Plant E.

The products produced in Plant D are considered semi-finished products or Work In Progress material.

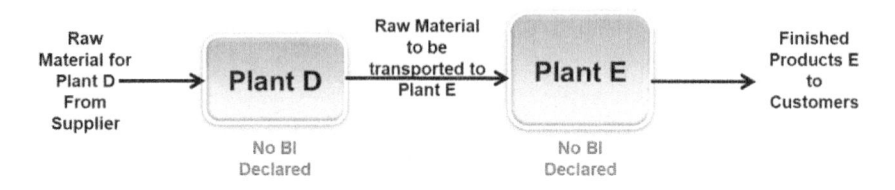

Raw Material for Plant D From Supplier → **Plant D** (No BI Declared) — Raw Material to be transported to Plant E → **Plant E** (No BI Declared) → Finished Products E to Customers

© Didier Schütz (DLS)

Depending on the layout of the two Plants D and E and on the chosen scenario, the BI loss could be very different:

- If the two Plants D and E are not adequately separated from a fire standpoint (i.e. Raw material stored on a 100m wide yard between the 2 plants and transported by lift-trucks, thus resulting in mutual exposure), a major fire starting at either Plant D or Plant E would spread to the other plant through the Raw Material yard storage providing fuel. In such a case the Extra Costs would rise to a total of USD 30 million (2xUSD 15 million per plant). This would further entail an Extra Cost for purchasing Finished Products on the market similar to those from Plant E in order to keep up supply to Customers.
- If, however, the two Plants D and E are well separated from a fire standpoint (i.e. Raw material from Plant D transported by truck to Plant E located 11km away):
  - In the case of a single event (i.e. natural perils such as windstorm) impacting the two plants, the Extra Costs would be the same as above (i.e. USD 30 million).
  - However, if a fire breaks out at either Plant D or Plant E, only one plant will be impacted and the extra cost would only be for purchasing Work In Progress material for Plant E should the loss occur at plant D or for processing

Work In Progress material from Plant D by a third party should the loss occur at Plant E.

Again, the above strategy for financing the induced BI is only valid if alternative supplier(s) is (are) already identified and contract(s) is (are) signed.

6. CONTINGENT BUSINESS INTERRUPTION (CBI) FOCUS

6.1. CBI Insurance Basics

This is an insurance policy that is beneficial if earnings are reduced because of damages to another business on which one's business is dependent. Contingent Business Interruption (CBI) insurance is an extension of other insurance cover that reimburses lost profits and extra expenses resulting from an interruption of business at the premises of a customer or supplier. CBI insurance is also known as Contingent Business Income insurance or Dependent Properties Insurance. Companies purchase this type of insurance as an extension to their standard property insurance.

There are four situations in which this cover is used:
- When the insured depends on a single supplier or a few suppliers for materials.
- When the insured depends on one or a few manufacturers or suppliers for most of its merchandise.
- When the insured depends on one or a few recipient businesses to purchase the bulk of the insured's products.
- When the insured counts on a neighboring business to help attract customers, known as a leader property.

The contingent property may be:

- Specifically named,

OR
- The cover may blanket all customers and suppliers.

6.2. CBI Insurance Across the World

CBI insurance is also known in Asia-Pacific as:
- "Contingent business income" insurance.
- "Dependent properties" insurance.

- "Waiting Hours" insurance
- "Time Deductibles" insurance

The term "Contingent Time Element" (CTE) is commonly used in the US:
- When discussing both CBI and contingent extra expense.
- A Time element simply refers to either:
Business Interruption
Or
Extra Expense cover (Extra Expense cover resulting from a contingent loss)

Other variations are observed across the world sometimes even in the same language and/or country:
- "Interruzione di servicio-Clausola Fornitori / Clienti" (Italian: extension of BI when declared as a % of PD).
- "Rückwirkungsschäden aus Betriebsunterbrechung" (German. Or CBI-Schäden).
- "Assurance Carence Client Fournisseur" (French).
- "Lucro Cesante Contingente" (Colombia).
- "Pérdidas por Paralización por failla de provedor / cliente" (chile).
- "Coberturas acumulación"; "Cadenas de suministros", "CBI's" (Spain).
- "Lucros Consequencial "(Mexico).
- "Lucro Cessante Contingente" (Brazilian).
- "Betinget Avbruddstap" (Norway).

6.3. Understanding CBI Insurance Cover

6.3.1. Governing perils

The most obvious difference between a CBI claim and a BI claim is that the insured is not dealing with damage to its facility and will not be handling a property damage claim.

It is very important to identify the underlying cover that triggers CBI. The following chain rule should apply for a BI cover to be triggered:

1. Physical Damage (PD) or Loss
2. To the property of the Supplier, Customer or Dependent property related to the Insured
3. Of the type covered as per the insurance policy of the Insured
4. Which causes an interruption to the Insured

As a result of the above, for the CBI insurance cover to apply, the type of physical damage must be the same as insured under the controlling policy (so called governing perils).

In order to provide adequate CBI insurance cover, the insured must identify and understand the impact of other businesses on his operations. This, of course, is not an easy task especially when the main suppliers are located thousands of miles away and when the main suppliers are replaced regularly with a cheaper option.

For example: A high tech company is located in the mountain area of Austria and is specialized in the production of surveillance drones. The risk finance program is a Property Insurance as per Named Perils (Fire, Earthquake and Flood) with extensions for BI and CBI.

- For the drone manufacturer in Austria, the sole supplier of the propeller micro electric driver is located in Indonesia in a coastal area subject to Tsunamis.

    Should a major **fire** destroy the unique supplier of the micro electric driver, located in Indonesia, the drone manufacturer in Austria would have to stop production sooner or later after consumption of all stock. The drone manufacturer can claim for CBI since the event impacting his supplier is of the type covered as per his Property insurance.

- However, should a **tsunami** destroy the unique supplier of the micro electric driver, located in Indonesia, the drone manufacturer in Austria would also have to stop production sooner or later after consumption of all stock. BUT the drone manufacturer CANNOT claim for CBI since the event impacting his supplier is NOT of the type covered as per his Property insurance.

6.3.2. Limits consideration

A dedicated limit (sub-limit) for CBI may be different than the one for BI. This limit is usually not higher than the BI limit.

Different sub limits can be considered for "Named" and "Un-named" suppliers / customers.

Moreover, the governing perils sub limits usually govern the CBI limit. Understanding the wording is key at this stage. The financial loss retained by the insured may, in some cases, be higher than the net loss of the insurance program. This would depend on the sub limit for a given event.

For example: An automotive manufacturer located in the US.
- The Insurance program of the automotive manufacturer is an All Risk type of Property Insurance excluding falling aircraft, wildfire and communicable diseases. There are also BI and CBI extensions.
- The sole supplier for the GPS is located in a country in Asia impacted by a flood due to heavy rainfall. The supplier's plant has not been operating for 4 months.
- The automotive manufacturer cannot equip any cars with GPS. This option is no longer available for the buyers and thus has an impact on sales.
- The automotive manufacturer in the US can claim for CBI due to a loss at its supplier's property in Asia caused by an event of the type covered (i.e. flood) in the automotive manufacturer Property Insurance.
- The Automotive manufacturer's loss of revenue is estimated at USD 1,000 million.
- However, the CBI has a lower limit than the BI as per the insurance cover: USD 500 million.

Moreover, the sub limit corresponding to the type of event must apply first: USD 100 million.

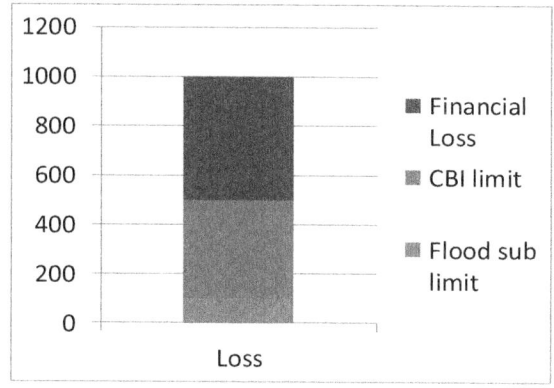

[Chart showing Loss with Financial Loss, CBI limit, and Flood sub limit, values up to 1000]

© Didier Schütz (DLS)

As a result of the above:
- Financial Loss: **USD 1,000 million**
- Net loss to the Insurance program: **USD 100 million**
- Financial loss retained by the Insured: **USD 900 million** (=1,000-100)

6.3.3. Typically, CBI Insurance is NOT a

- Utility service interruption or an off-premises power interruption.
- Civil or military authority interruption.
- Lack of ingress or egress interruption.
- "Interdependency or downstream business interruption, when damage at an owned location causes a loss of revenue to another owned location" (interdependences).
- Loss which results from a change in temperature due to damage to heating or cooling equipment.

Warning:
- The wording of the CBI insurance cover is key.
- It may differ from one country to another. The UK tends to strictly stick to its own definition. The US, European market and Asia tend to have a more flexible approach on the subject. Hence, Supply Interruption may be considered as CBI if utilities are defined as being the same as any other supplies.

6.3.4. Strange CBI Insurance cover

The two following examples were noticed during on-site risk inspections in the presence of the finance and insurance department. Somehow, the purpose of the cover had not been properly understood.

Example 1:
- A food processing plant purchasing CBI cover for the loss of "named suppliers". When asking for the list of suppliers we were provided with a page where only the title "List of Suppliers" was visible.

Example 2:
- A Renewal Energy company with several wind farms in the same country purchasing CBI cover for the loss of supplier but with a higher limit than its BI limit.
- The main customer of a wind farm is usually the national grid.
- However, it is actually very complicated to identify the main supplier of a wind farm (i.e. wind provider).
- Some external electric power may be needed for the control systems but this should be considered as utilities thus no longer falling under CBI but under SI (service Interruption).
- In any case, it is difficult to imagine what could justify a higher limit for CBI/SI than the BI itself.

6.4. Supply Chain Vs CBI

A supply chain is a network between a company and its suppliers to produce and distribute a specific product to the final buyer. This network includes different activities, people, entities, information, and resources. The supply chain also encompasses the steps necessary to get the product or service from its original state to the customer.

The steps include moving and transforming raw materials into finished products, transporting those products and distributing them to the end-user. The entities involved in the supply chain include producers, vendors, warehouses, transportation companies, distribution centers, and retailers but also any entities helping to attract, please and keep the client thanks to additional services.

Supply chain management is a crucial process because an optimized supply chain results in lower costs and a faster production cycle.

For a given organization, the supply chain can be summarized using 3 main entities as follows:
- **The Supplier(s)** providing Raw Material, equipment, services.
- **The Customer(s)** receiving the Finished Products, goods.
- **After Sales & Services**: anything that keeps the business going (e.g. shopping area, sales platform, show room, permanent/temporary exhibition center, e-marketing, customer service, testing lab. / center, delivery, warranty, pick-up, returns, hot line, support / services package, repair, exchange, alternative solutions, e-user manual, financing solutions, etc.).

Financing the risks of an Organization in terms of Property Damage and Business Interruption may also include a CBI extension that covers any failure of the main entities of the supply chain above. For such CBI insurance cover, the following insurance terminology applies:
- **The Supplier(s)** = CBI Contributing Property
- **The Customer(s)** = CBI Recipient Property
- **After Sales & Services** = Leader Property

Virtual examples and real cases are given by way of illustration in the following sub-sections.

6.4.1. CBI Contributing Property

Example 1: the Insured is a Tractor Manufacturer for farmers.
- The Tractor Manufacturer is insured for Property Damage for the following named perils: fire, flood, wind. There are also

extensions for BI and CBI (same limits) for suppliers and customers.
- The rubber tires are supplied by a sole supplier located in the same region, thus reducing the delivery time and allowing for prompt technical support when needed.
- Last Friday the rubber tire supplier's plant was destroyed by a fire. The plant will be out of operation for at least 12 months.
- The Tractor Manufacturer has buffer storage of 4 months production on its premises.
- Other potential suppliers for rubber tires are identified and contacts are established and signed. These suppliers are located overseas and at least 6 months will be needed for restoring the delivery of tires to a full production situation.
- The loss at the supplier property is of the type (i.e. fire) covered by the Property Insurance of the Tractor Manufacturer.
- The Tractor Manufacturer could claim for CBI because of having lost its supplier leading to at least 2 months BI which corresponds to the time elapsed between the use of the last tire available from the buffer storage and the resumption of production at the same capacity as before the loss but with tires delivered by the external suppliers. Loss of revenue (margin) may also be claimed under the same CBI cover due to the difference of costs (if any) for the rubber tires delivered from overseas. On the other hand, in the case of a better deal for the tires delivered from overseas, no additional claims would be justified.

Example 2: B Automotive Loss, Central Europe
- B Automotive is a company specializing in the production and commercialization of cars' elastomer interior (instrument panels, dashboard skins and door panels).
- It directly serves Western Europe based car manufacturers, as well as Original Equipment Manufacturers (OEM) in the automotive sector.
- Initial event: On Sunday, a severe fire incident occurred in one of the production halls of B Automotive's Central Europe Automotive Interiors subsidiary.

- B Automotive advised that this plant is the sole worldwide provider of patented polyurethane sprayed skins for car interiors.
- Some specific moulds for door panels belonging to the manufacturers were destroyed.
- The day after on Monday, B Automotive announced that following the fire the premises were closed by the authorities for safety reasons, and production had been stopped.
- Loss assessment was around € 340 million for automotive manufacturers.

Example 3: "North America based Automotive Manufacturer suspends production of famous trucks"

- North America based Automotive Manufacturer suspends production of its Famous trucks after a fire at a supplier's facility caused it to run out of parts for the nation's best-selling vehicle.
- The famous truck has been the top selling North American vehicle by any manufacturer for more than 40 years.
- The shutdowns could last for several weeks.
- North America based Automotive Manufacturer has about an 84-day supply of the Famous-Series truck in dealers' inventories, according to the company. That's sufficient for there to be no shortages in the near term.
- But if the shutdown lasts a month, buyers may discover that the version of the truck they want — the type of engine or the type of cab configuration or trim — won't be available.
- Those shortages are typical when vehicle inventory falls below 50 days.
- The precarious situation "demonstrates the riskier side of North America based Automotive Manufacturer 's strategy to put all its eggs in the trucks and SUVs basket."

6.4.2. CBI Recipient Property

Example: The Chain Saw Engine Manufacturer.

- This Chain Saw Engine Manufacturer is producing only one type of product (i.e. low level of diversification, high level of specialization) purchased by only two Customers A and B, respectively representing 75% and 25% of its BI.
- The Chain Saw Engine Manufacturer is insured for Property Damages upon All Risks policy excluding Flood, Communicable Diseases and Cyber. There are also extensions for BI and CBI (same limits) for suppliers and customers.
- Customer A, located near a major river, is flooded. Reinstatement of premises is taking 5 months.
- In the meantime, for 5 months the Chain Saw Engine Manufacturer cannot deliver its products to Customer A. This represents 75% of its revenue.
- The loss at the supplier property is NOT of the type (flood is excluded) covered by the Property Insurance of the Chain Saw Manufacturer.
- The Tractor Manufacturer CANNOT claim for CBI for the loss of its Customer A.

See example 2 below - BCN Indus. within TCC below for CBI Leader Property also covering CBI Recipient Property.

6.4.3. CBI Leader Property

Example 1: the Insured is a Bakery located within a shopping mall housing a hypermarket:

- The Bakery is insured for Property Damages for the following named perils: fire and explosion. There are also extensions for BI and CBI (same limits) including all 3 components: Contributing, Recipient and Leader Property.

- The revenue of this bakery is linked to the fact that the customers buying bread and pastries are mainly those shopping at the hypermarket.
- During Sunday night, a major fire severely damaged the storage area of the hypermarket which was closed for investigation, cleaning and reinstatement for 6 months.
- The loss at the hypermarket attracting clients (i.e. Leader Property) is of the type (fire) covered by the Property Insurance of the Tractor Manufacturer.
- The bakery submitted a CBI claim for the loss of the Leader Property. The loss of revenue was in the range of 85% during the 6 months.

Note:
- The leader property is also called "Anchor" store (Canada) or Magnet Store (US) in the case of a neighboring business (e.g. shopping mall) that attracts customers.
- The loss of Leader Property is sometimes insured under a dedicated cover for "loss of attraction" (see other contingency extensions section).

Example 2: BCN Indus. within the Trade Center Complex (TCC)
- The insured, BCN Indus., provided extensive engineering and janitorial services at the Trade Center Complex (TCC).
- BCN Indus. operated the HVAC system (Heat Ventilation and Air Conditioning) for the entire complex and provided janitorial services for the public areas as well as for most tenants.
- BCN Indus. employed over 800 people who worked at the Trade Center Complex.
- BCN Indus. created a call center in the Trade Center Complex for tenants to report problems and developed preventative maintenance schedules with state-of-the-art software that tracked the equipment in the Trade Center Complex.
- The Insurance Policy issued to BCN Indus. included BI, CBI.
- This policy also insures against loss resulting from damage to or destruction by causes of loss insured against, to property not owned or operated by the Insured, located in the same vicinity as the Insured, which attracts business to the Insured.

- Further to the destruction of the Trade Center Complex (TCC), BCN Indus. submitted claims to the Insurer under the BI cover.
- The Insurer contended that the claimed damages were covered only under the CBI cover (limit of USD 10 million) and that no cover was available under BI, leader property and civil authority provisions.
- With regard to contingent business income cover, the Court first determined that because BCN Indus. used and "operated" the Trade Center Complex (TCC), it was not a dependent property.
- BCN Indus. asserted its loss of business income from the destruction of the Trade Center Complex (TCC) were covered by the Leader Property provision.
- The court then analyzed the meaning of attraction property and stated: We reject the notion that a property cannot "attract" business to another entity at the same site or adjacent to it". Nonetheless, we conclude that Leader Property cover was appropriate in this case.

6.5. CBI Impact

The impact related to the loss of supplier, customer or leader property is different from one organization to another. However, the following main trends are observed.

Contingent Business Interruption	Impact
Contributing Property (Contributing Supplier / Manufacturer)	High to Very High (few or no back up capability available and multiple tiers involved)
Recipient Property (Customer)	Low to Medium (when products can be re-directed)
Leader Property (attracting customer)	Very Low to Low (considering potential relocation, redundancy)

Warning: the above severity rates are only indicative and based on loss history and current conditions that may change in the future or for some cases. This should be investigated in detail for a given case.

6.6. CBI Tiers Factor

The position of the suppliers and customers inside the supply chain is very important in terms of CBI cover. The position is referred to as a "Tier" as shown below.

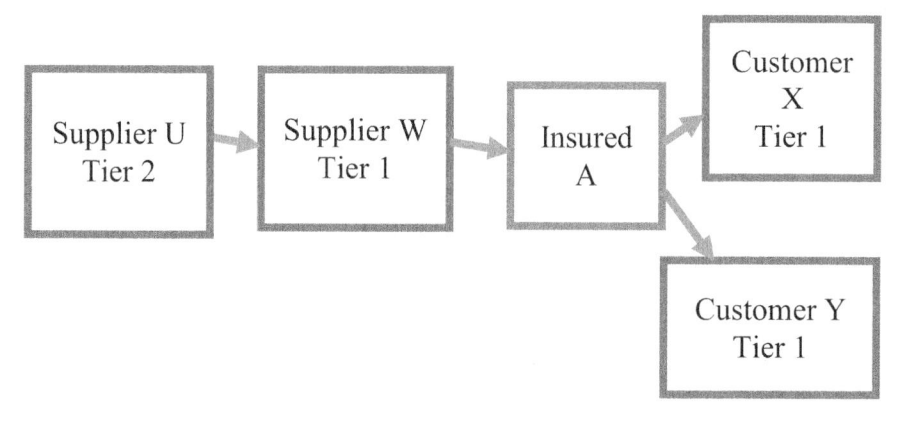

```
[Supplier U    →  [Supplier W    →  [Insured   →  [Customer X
 Tier 2]           Tier 1]            A]             Tier 1]
                                        ↓
                                     [Customer Y
                                      Tier 1]
```

© Didier Schütz (DLS)

The following limitations / precisions or a combination in terms of "Tier" can be found in CBI Insurance cover:
- "Direct" suppliers & customers (i.e. "Tier 1")
- "Indirect" suppliers & customers (i.e. Tier 2, 3, 4…)
- Named suppliers & customers (regardless of the Tier)
- Unnamed suppliers & customers (regardless of the Tier)

Different limits and deductibles can also be applied to the CBI insurance cover depending on Tier, named or unnamed.

6.7. CBI (Re)Insurance Purpose

6.7.1. The fire that changed the Industry

The following Loss occurred in year 2000 and has become the classic case of supply chain disruption.

This was deemed as the fire that changed the Industry of semiconductors and electronics.

Electronic Cy Loss - Southwestern region of the USA:
- The microchip was a fast growing market: the mobile phone market was growing 40% per annum. Component makers were working at full capacity with a very high demand from consumer electronic companies (virtually at any price). There was a shortage of components.
- Electronic Cy, at the time of the Loss, was a leading-edge technology company. It had acquired several plants and had boosted its production capacity 40% compared to 1999 levels. 17 plants were churning out 80 million chips a day used in 80% of the mobile phones sold worldwide. In year 2000 the chip volume grew 33% and revenue 55%. Electronic Cy simply had no surplus capacity.
- The US Electronic Cy plant located in Southwestern region of the USA was a radio frequency chip manufacturing plant.
- At 8pm a lightning bolt struck a high voltage electricity line in the Southwestern region of the USA resulting in power fluctuations across the state.
- Due to the power fluctuations a fire broke out in a manufacturing line of the US Electronic Cy plant radio frequency chip manufacturing plant in Southwestern region of the USA.
- Sprinklers were activated, plant personnel reacted quickly. The fire was extinguished within 10 minutes.
- The first investigation showed: 8 trays of silicon wafers destroyed by fire on that line. Damage was limited to Work In Progress material (USD 40 million) corresponding to several thousand cell phones when fully processed.
- Deeper investigation showed: smoke & water had contaminated millions of chips stored for shipment (Finished Products).

- Chip factory production was carried out under "clean-room" conditions (10,000 times cleaner than in hospital). Several tridimensional printed circuits were printed and embedded in a surface as small as a baby's finger nails. The cleanup was expected to take at least a week (USD 39Mo cost).
- Electronic Cy was the supplier for critical components (i.e. Radio Frequency Chips) to different mobile phone manufacturers of which two leaders respectively located in Suomi Northern Europe and in Scandinavia, located more than 5,000 miles away. Suomi Mobile Phone and Scandinavia Mobile Phone represented 40% of Electronic' plant shipment.
- Electronic Cy called their customers on March 20: "they may be temporarily impacted, and their orders would be filled first when the plant returned to normal".
- Five years before the shortfall at US Electronic Cy plant, Suomi Mobile Phone had put in place a chips inflow management system (planners) making it possible to detect potential chip supply chain disruptions from Electronic Cy before being officially informed. Once informed by Electronic Cy, Suomi Mobile Phone expected cleanup could take more than one week. The Suomi culture being one of those that encourages discussing possible problems openly, Suomi Mobile Phone took 3 key steps very rapidly:
  - One team developed alternative plans with Electronic Cy rearranging its plans in other sister factories worldwide (e.g. Continental Europe, Asia).
  - A second cross continental team redesigned some chips so that they could be produced in other Electronic Cy (coordinating with) and non- Electronic Cy plants.
  - A third group worked to find alternative manufacturers to reduce pressure on Electronic Cy (2 suppliers responded within 5 days).
- Before Electronic Cy' call, Scandinavian Mobile Phone had not sensed any discrepancy in Electronic Cy' performance. Scandinavian Mobile Phone, meanwhile, had accepted early assurances that the fire was unlikely to cause a big problem and settled down to wait it out. Moreover, Scandinavian Mobile Phone a few years earlier, had decided to buy key components from a single source to simplify its supply chain.

- Two weeks after the loss Electronic Cy communicated to their clients on the loss development as summarized below:
  - Existing stock of Chips contaminated by smoke and could not be sent to the customers.
  - Loss of production: 100% for 13 days (longer cleaning period than expected).
  - Gradually restoration to full production in 6 weeks.
- When they realized their mistake, it was too late. Scandinavian Mobile Phone was not able to find alternative suppliers for the Radio Frequency Chips on time and experimented Business Interruption and loss of market share. Single sourcing may have its benefits, but it also has its costs:
  - Scandinavian Mobile Phone lost many months of production, and hence many sales (# USD 430-570 million).
  - in a booming market that was therefore dominated by Suomi Mobile Phone (loss of market share # 3% # USD 2.34 billion).
  - Scandinavian Mobile Phone returned to health in 2004. (Revenues had fallen 52%).

- Scandinavian Mobile Phone learned its lesson and now has a completely different supply chain risk management system in place including but not limited to:
  - <u>Vulnerabilities Identification</u>: mapping all the key components and products many tiers upstream in the supply chain. They identify critical suppliers and sites that have to be prioritized and further assessed.
  - <u>Vulnerability Assessment</u>: rough assessment on how shortage will affect the supply chain, more thorough investigation into probability and impact of different accidents at different suppliers is conducted to assess the impact on the supply chain as a whole, particularly the impact on business recovery time.
  - <u>Risk Response</u>: Finally, Risk Management actions (protection) are evaluated against risk costs (impact and consequences), to avoid over-action or over-insurance against incidents.

After this loss CBI became a great concern for the (Re)Insurance Industry.

- Cover of CBI or unlimited suppliers extension at the time of the loss exposed the (Re)Insurers to an unknown accumulation
- This could result in multiple loss exposure from one single incident (independent of the geographic location) with a multitude of claims notifications.
- Reinsurers are exponentially more exposed to this risk than any ceding insurer.
- To control such a multitude of exposures it appeared fundamental to have each and every supplier named in the policy, which includes the suppliers extension.
- Since the above is not always practical, a sub-limit for the extended cover for suppliers is at least a mitigating element.

6.7.2. The goldfish syndrome

A good friend of mine in China once told me that goldfish, even in a very small aquarium, are never depressed, the secret being their so-called "flash memory" limited to only 7 seconds. As a result, endlessly swimming in circles is no problem as they re-discover their bowl each time around.

© Franck Orset (FPO)

It seems that this same syndrome is widespread for CBI.

For each and every new event generating a major disruption of the supply chain of a given or multiple industry sectors, the impacts in terms of CBI seem to be discovered each time as if for the first time.

Examples of major supply chain disruptions having a strong impact on CBI are not numerous yet regularly recorded. We just need to remind ourselves of the following golden rules:
- CBI Risk exists
- This is not an Emerging Risk
- This is a Latent Risk regularly emerging

CBI losses resulting from major events disrupting the supply chain have been recorded:
- 1999 Taiwan EQ
- 2000 Electronic Cy - Scandinavian Mobile Phone - Suomi Mobile Phone (see 6.7.1).
- 2008 Australia Gas supply
- 2011 WTC 9/11
- 2011/02 Japan Earthquake
- 2011/09 Thai flood

6.7.3. Stress Test for the Global economy

Considering the current "Global Economy" involving "Global Interactions", any large scale events create an opportunity for large scale BI and CBI losses to aggregate.

The fundamental criteria for such critical CBI aggregation can be summarized with the following 3-step chain rule:
1. Industry sector(s) sensitive to any supply chain disruption.
2. Business Units all concentrated in one area.
3. The area is possibly Exposed to Large Scale Perils.

One of the most relevant examples is the automotive industry sector in Asia - Pacific:

1. Organized on platforms with partners and various multiple tier suppliers.
2. Japanese Original Equipment Manufacturers (OEMs) dominating the South-East Asian market.
3. South East Asia is an area subject to strong Earthquake, Tsunami and Typhoons.

The same can be observed with the semiconductor (chips) industry:

1. Multiple step industry sectors fragmented with various producers mutually interacting.
2. Regional concentration in the so called Silicon Sea-Belt from Japan to Singapore including Foundries, Testing and Assembly facilities (e.g. Japan providing more than 50% of the global supply of semiconductor wafers. Thailand is responsible for the manufacturing of about ¼ of all Hard Disk Drives supplying the global computing industry). R&D mostly made in Western Europe and Western USA.
3. The Silicon Sea-Belt is an area subject to strong Earthquake, Tsunami and Typhoons.

As a matter of fact:

- Modern organizations (ZOOG oriented – see section 1.3) are more sensitive to:
    - Large scale natural Perils (e.g. Hurricane Katrina, Volcano in Iceland, powerful quake in Japan, flood in Thailand, etc.)
    - Man-made perils (WTC 9/11, Iraq, Afghanistan, Syria, Libya …).
    - Worldwide Instability (Financial & political crisis….).
    - Social Unrest (Northern Africa, Europe).
    - Energy & environmental considerations.
    - Pandemic.
    - Etc.

- The assembly type occupancy sectors (e.g. automotive, electronics) are usually more sensitive to supply chain disruption than manufacturing or primary production sectors (e.g. mining, metal industry). However, large losses and potential accumulations of BI and CBI cannot be excluded.
- Sectors with High Exposure include, but are not limited to:
    o   Pharmaceutical.
    o   Automotive, Aerospace & Defense.
    o   Semiconductors, Electronics.
    o   Telecom.
- The type of CBI Exposure includes but is not limited to:
    o   Joint Ventures with "competitors" for products.
    o   Active Ingredient Suppliers.
    o   Packaging (PS preforms, Blisters, etc.).
    o   Raw Materials, spares with long lead time.
    o   Suppliers, customers (sole, major, no alternatives).
    o   Qualification, Certification, Approval (Federal Aviation Agency, Food and Drug Administration, etc.).

6.7.4. Need for Managing CBI Accumulation

At the Re-insurance level, it is very important to be able to manage potential CBI accumulation resulting from one single event somewhere in the world impacting one or more industry sector(s) across the globe. This is necessary in order to do the following (amongst other things):

- Control the Magnitude of Potential Loss Exposure (crossed CBI, Unknown suppliers....).
- Optimize Retrocession.
- Produce Critical Data for Further Retrocession purposes in the case of a Loss.

However, at the Reinsurance level the Detection of any latent critical CBI risk aggregation can only be adequately done if based on accurate data received from the insured via the insurers (so called ceding Cy) who are the ones with direct access to the insured risks.

Understanding the supply chain (Suppliers, Products, area) based on accurate data received from the insured is the main challenge for the insurance industry.

However, (Re)insurance Companies may try to manage their accumulations (also called aggregates) they are not responsible for securing the Supply Chain of the insured.

Securing the supply chain is the responsibility of the Risk Management teams. However, in actual fact, Organizations have problems in identifying and managing their supply chain above Tier 1. Even simply identifying the supplier (Tier 2) of the direct supplier (Tier 1) of an Organization may be quite challenging. Moreover, the tier 2 supplier can change without any prior notice.

6.7.5. CBI Claims development

CBI Claims development is usually longer than the BI claims development as shown in the following example. This could be like a "time bomb" for a (Re)Insurance company.

Example: strong winds hit unloading facilities (cranes) located and belonging to a Harbor Company.

© Franck Orset (FPO)

These unloading facilities are used to import coal for the nearest integrated steel mill complex. The coal is used as a Raw Material to produce Iron within a blast furnace.
Part of the off gases from the process are re-injected into the process for better efficiency and the production of electricity is used at the site but also sold on the market (excess).

- The cranes having been destroyed by the windstorm, coal had to be imported from another berth with smaller capacity. This was arranged by the Harbor Company in order to ensure business continuity.
- This had a negative impact on the process of the steel mill itself but also on the availability of electric power that had to be purchased from the grid, resulting in extra costs and loss of revenue (no excess of power to be sold to the grid).
- The two sites (Harbor Company and the Integrated Steel Mills) were insured by the same insurance company so the following BI and CBI claims accumulated with the same insurer (see table):

Unloading Facility Belonging to Harbor Cy	Steel Making Cy (SMC) (25 months after Harbor Cy claim)
Property Damages to cranes, conveyor, jetty **Extra costs** for using other berths to unload coal and road / rail transportation to client	**Demurrage** (*) **Loss of sales** of FP (steel) due to the lack of coal Extra cost for buying Finished Products for a major customer Loss of sale for a sister plant producing for a major customer **Loss of energy generation** due to process slow down due to the lack of coal resulting in lack of off gases, loss of process efficiency and loss of electricity sale and extra cost to purchase electric power **Extra cost** for delivery of coal from other berths using smaller ships (higher cost) and road / rail transportation and buffer storage areas. Taxed paid on higher production rate **Other**…
PD: USD 110 million BI & Extra Cost: USD 50-100 million	CBI: USD 135-200 million Including loss of sales, Extra costs

(*) charge payable to the owner of a chartered ship on failure to load or discharge the ship within the time agreed

7. SERVICE INTERRUPTION (SI) FOCUS

7.1. SI Definition

Service Interruption may be defined as an accidental failure of supply. However, this is too simple and not sufficiently accurate for (Re)Insurance purposes.

It is very important to define what kinds of "Services" are considered.

© Franck Orset (FPO)

The term "Facility Services Interruption" can also be used.

"Facility Services" can be provided in many forms including but not limited to:
- Electric Power
- Fuel (gas, oil, coal)
- Steam (process, utilities, heating)
- Air (compressed, air separation unit)
- Air treatment, Air cond., special atmosphere, emission treatment
- Water (treatment, supply, cooling)
- Effluent (treatment, cooling, sewage)
- Chemicals (liquid, solid, gaseous)
- Transportation (ground, air, conveyors)

- Communications (telephone, data transmission)
- Security (on-site or remote central station)
- Refrigeration (unit, fluid)

7.2. SI Loss Magnitude

Catastrophic losses such as natural perils often shut down power and utility services for weeks over a wide territory which has a major impact on people's lives and also on many businesses. These very critical utilities are also called "lifelines".

A major incident such as a fire or explosion impacting the nearest power station of the gas supplier may also have considerable impact over a wide area on various businesses of different sizes and class occupancies such as:

- An aluminum smelter: solidification of aluminum within the potline (so called "pot freeze") leading to USD 200 million Property loss and from 8 up to 18 months Business Interruption because of the reinstatement period extending far beyond the restoration of the electric power supply.
- The food in the refrigerators spoils and a restaurant is unable to serve customers for several days, possibly even longer considering the necessary cleaning and sanitizing period.
- A brewery using water supplied from a private water treatment plant can be contaminated. All batches of brewing beer could be lost, representing several hectoliters, and all brewing equipment would need to be cleaned before restarting the brewery several weeks later.
- A hotel located in a remote location can be out of business for a relatively long time when that remote location is subject to hurricanes that may damage the 50km long single overhead feeder supplying electric power.
- The rupture of a main process water pipe supplying a mine in a very cold country during winter time can only be repaired during the summer. In the mean-time the ore processing plant will have to stop operations.

According to a study over a period of 20 years (1990-2010) in Northern America, the causes and consequences of service interruption for small and medium sized businesses are the following:

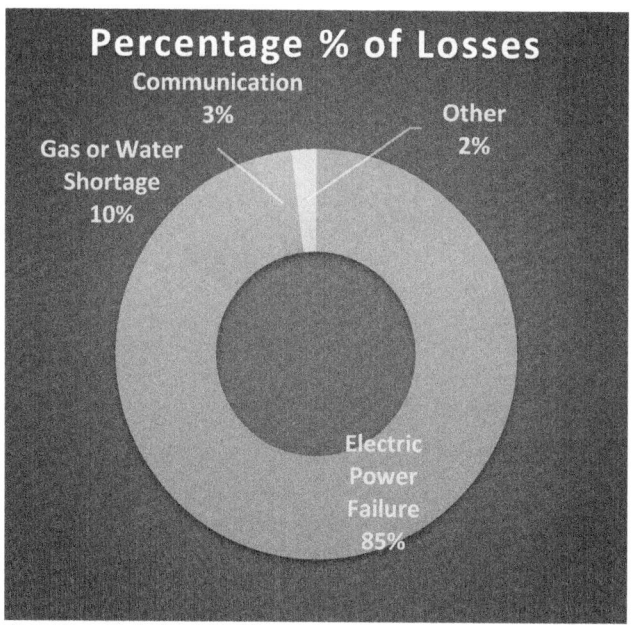

Percentage % of Losses
- Communication 3%
- Other 2%
- Gas or Water Shortage 10%
- Electric Power Failure 85%

© Didier Schütz (DLS)

Consequences of Electric Power Failure recorded for the same period for small and medium size businesses:

- Spoilage due to loss of refrigeration:
    - 60% of it considered as Property Damage.
    - 40% related to time-element.

- Equipment/material contamination losses:
    - 33% of Property Damage.
    - 67% time element related.

7.3. SI Insurance needs

Certain businesses are at greater risk of financial difficulty than others should utilities fail:
- Businesses located in a geographical area known to be exposed to devastating natural perils
- Utility services known to be non-reliable and/or a long time needed for reinstatement in case of a major loss and/or there is no alternative supply.
- Businesses sensitive to the loss of a utility service (e.g. electricity, gas, water) so that any outage would lead to financial loss (i.e. damage to processing equipment, loss of Work In Progress material or perishable goods).

In order to provide adequate SI insurance cover, the insured must identify and understand the impact of utility service providers on his operations. This, of course, is not always an easy task. It is all about Risk Management.

For example:
- Telecommunication services may be very critical for an IT facility for a short period of time and less critical for a steel mill.
- The loss of electric power for 5 hours may be very critical for some heavy industries resulting in a large loss but less critical for a hotel.

Some commercial property policies may clearly exclude property damage or loss due to utility failure. In these situations, "Utility Service Interruption Coverage" (or "SI") is needed.

However, Utility Service Interruption Coverage cannot usually be purchased as a stand-alone policy as it serves to close the gap left by utility exclusions listed in most commercial property policies.

Utility Service Interruption Coverage is therefore commonly added as an endorsement to commercial property and business income policies, addressing the utility exclusions that are included in most property policies.

7.4. SI Insurance Across the World

In British English it appears that Service Interruption only include utilities (i.e. "Utility Service Interruption").

In other countries and other languages, utility providers may not be distinguished from any other suppliers (i.e. Raw Material, Packaging). As a result, interruption of utilities or SI may be included or even combined in the generic CBI cover without distinction.

Just keep in mind that the insurance industry can be very creative (see extent of coverage below).

7.5. Understanding SI Insurance Cover

7.5.1. Extent of coverage

The extent of coverage depends on many of the details chosen in the endorsements such as the type of "Facility services" as described above or even more accurately defined by the types of "Utility Property" the Organization wants to insure based on risk analysis.

The main types of "Utility Property" include:
- Water: Pumping stations and water mains.
- Communications: Telephone, radio, internet, microwave, and television services, including satellite dishes, optic fiber transmission lines, coaxial cables, and overhead lines (*).
- Power: Properties supplying electricity, steam, or gas, including generating plants, switching stations, substations, transformers, and overhead Transmission and Distribution – T&D- lines (*).

(*) Note that overhead lines (i.e. Telecom lines, power Transmission and Distribution -T&D – lines) aren't typically automatically covered by insurance companies or only a section extending to some hundreds of meters or a few kms from the premises of the insured may be covered.

Typical perils considered for the SI cover often mimic the perils covered by the Property policy cover of the Insured and may include:
- Fire
- Lightning
- Wind
- Hail
- Explosion

However, the "Utility Property" may be exposed to different perils than those covered by the Property policy cover of the Insured. For example: The insured operates a large scale Industrial Chocolate factory. The Property cover is limited to Fire, Lightning, Explosion.
- Most of the equipment within the Industrial Chocolate Factory is either electricity driven or electrically power heated.
- Any electricity power outage of more than 6 hours would result in the loss of heat for the processing equipment causing the liquid chocolate to solidify plugging all conduits and leading to an at least 1 month Business Interruption for cleaning as well as the loss of tons of Work In Progress materials.
- The sole electricity supplier operates a thermal power plant located at the end of the runway of the international airport and supplies the Industrial Chocolate Factory through a 15km long overhead Transmission & Distribution line.
- In such a case it is better to have "Falling Aircraft" peril considered for the SI cover.

The "Insured Property" to be covered against damage or loss due to utility interruption at the insured facility should also be well defined. For example:
- Any property,
- Including buildings,
- Including contents,
- Including third parties' properties located within the insured property,
- etc.

"Utility Service Interruption Coverage" typically provides cover for either or both of the two following types of losses:

- Direct Damage: covers loss or damage to the insured property caused by an interruption to utility services.
- Business Interruption with Time Element: covers loss of business income or extra expense coverage to cover any losses in income or incurred extra expenses due to a suspension of business operations caused by an interruption to utility services.

The most obvious difference between a CBI claim and a SI claim is that the insured may also have Property Damage to its facility because of the failure of utility supplies (i.e. power outage leading to the spoiling of perishable food in a freezer or damage to equipment in a heavy industry due to an uncontrolled shut down or solidification of molten metal).

7.5.2. Governing Perils

Utility Service Interruption Coverage (or SI), also known as off-premises power coverage, protects businesses from property damage and loss due to utility failure, originating away from the premises of the insured property, **caused by a covered peril** (as described below).

Utility Service Interruption Coverage (or SI) can cover direct damage to property, losses in income, and extra expenses incurred to keep the business of the insured running in the event of a utility failure **caused by a covered peril** (as described below).

It is therefore very important to identify the underlying cover that has triggered the SI. The following chain rule should apply for BI cover to be triggered:

1. Physical Damage (PD) or Loss
2. To the property of the utility service provider supplying the Insured
3. Of the type covered as per the insurance policy of the Insured
4. Which causes an interruption to the Insured

As a result of the above for the SI insurance cover to apply, the type of physical damage must be the same as is insured under the controlling policy (so called governing perils)

The utility service provider may be

- Specifically named,

OR

- The cover may blanket all service providers (when multiple) for a given type of utility.

7.5.3. Limits consideration

A dedicated limit (sub-limit) for SI may be different to the BI one. This limit is not usually higher than the BI limit.

Different sub limits can be considered for "Named" and "Unnamed" utility service providers.

Moreover, the governing perils sub limits usually govern the SI limit (similar to the CBI case).

Understanding the wording is key at this stage. The financial loss retained by the insured can be higher than the net loss of the insurance program in some cases depending on sub limits for a given event.

For example: A Distribution Center located in an island in the Pacific Ocean specializes in the import, storage and distribution of perishable goods (i.e. frozen food, fresh vegetables / meat / fish).

- All perishable goods are stored in sub-freezing temperature cold rooms. The Distribution Center is in fact a giant fridge.
- The refrigeration system in the cold room includes electric driven compressors and a loop of ammonia-based refrigeration fluid.

- Electric power is fed through a single overhead distribution line to the Distribution Center from the sole power station of the island located 30km away on the other side of a chain of mountains. There are no alternative electric power sources. The grid is known to be non-reliable due to the lack of investment and growing demand.
- In the case of an electric power blackout exceeding 8 hours all perishable goods would be lost. The site is equipped with Diesel Engine Driven Emergency Generators providing up to 48 hours electric power for the cold rooms. At least 2 power outages not exceeding 4 hours are reported every month.
- The Insurance program of the Distribution Center is an All Risk type of Property Insurance excluding flood and cyber. The Risk Manager purchased the following cover with limits based on a risk benefit analysis (the type of business and the risk of loss associated with it greatly impacts the cost of the premium and policy. Generally, the premium will increase if there is a high chance of an incident occurring due to a covered peril):
    - Wind is sub-limited to € 10 million (out of € 200 million PD value): the building includes a wind design compliant with international standards factoring in extra tropical windstorm exposure.
    - BI extension up to € 40 million limit (corresponding to 1 year BI).
    - CBI extension for named suppliers up to € 10 million.
    - SI extension for electric power limited to € 20 million (based on 4 months Business Interruption foreseen in the case of a major loss impacting the national grid and Property Damages limited to spoiled goods and disposal, cold room cleaning and sanitizing costs).
- The island was hit by Typhoon Wendy severely damaging homes and infrastructures including the destruction of two thirds of the overhead lines and pylons supplying the distribution Center. The Distribution Center itself was not damaged.
- The reinstatement of the overhead distribution line won't take place for a year. The resources of the national grid company are limited and focused on top priorities such as residential

areas, health care facilities, water treatment plants, etc. In the meantime, the Distribution Center has been shut down.
- The loss of revenue for the Distribution Center is therefore € 40 million due to SI.
- The SI has a limit of € 20 million
- Moreover, the sub-limit for this type of event applies: € 10 million.
- As a result of the above:
    - Financial Loss: € 40 million
    - Net loss to the Insurance program: € 10 million (due to wind: governing peril)
    - Financial loss retained by the Insured: € 30 million (=40-10)

7.6. SI Loss Experiences

1998 - Ice Storm – North America

Event:
- Freezing rain
- Duration 5 days
- 100 millimeters (4 inches) of ice deposited

Ice storm 98 Meteorological factors:
- 3 day's advance warning but duration not predicted
- Jet stream: atypical paths leading to freezing rain
- El Niño: aggravating factor

Impact:
- Ice 4 to 5 times the weight of cables (17 times the local standards design parameters).

Consequences:
- Close to 110,000 homes, farms and businesses ("customers") were without electricity.

- 1.4 million customers lost power – translating into roughly three million people or half the province's population.
- Municipalities and townships in the affected area declared a state of emergency and the federal government mobilized over 15,500 soldiers in the biggest peacetime deployment of the Armed Forces in the country's history.
- 1,000 impairments due to power outages were reported including but not limited to:
  - Bridges and roads closed
  - Water filtration plants down
  - Telephone service significantly impaired
  - Fire alarm system dysfunctional
  - Dry pipe valve compressors and fire pump issue (electric heat tracer) impaired
  - Sprinkler system freeze
  - Frozen food spoilage
  - Freezing of perishable products
- Insurance and reinsurance aspects of the storm:
  - Restoration of electric power in 26 days
  - Insured Loss USD 1 billion
  - Number of Claims 665,000
  - Myriad social, political and business pressures
- Policy wordings don't always provide the clear-cut answers everyone is looking for.
  - How should the Additional Living Expenses (ALE) section respond if there is no damage to the property in question?
  - Did the insureds take proper measures to mitigate or prevent losses?
  - Insurers said they would consider a call by Provin's Premier for people to leave their unheated homes as the equivalent of an evacuation order. This allowed for additional

living expense claims to be recognized in the absence of physical damage to insured property. (Mass evacuation by virtue of civil authority).

- Personal lines (PL) policies - Issues:
  - Personal lines (PL) policies tend to be similar but not identical.
  - Most large insurers have their own forms and although the Insurance Bureau has a standard PL wording,
  - It was not readily known at the time of this event just how many insurers used it.
- Commercial covers for business interruption and liability questions:
  - At the time of the storm, most commercial policies provided coverage on a broad form (all risks) basis with only a minority being written on the old fire and extended cover basis.
  - In perhaps 50% of policies a form of business interruption coverage (loss of income) was included.
  - As a general rule if there is no damage to the insured property there is no business interruption loss.
  - At the time of this storm there were some exceptions: a number of large firms (particularly manufacturing and processing risks) bought cover for 'off-premise power.' In the event of a shut down due to interruption of the power supply by an insured peril, BI coverage would respond.
  - The more common forms of business interruption provide coverage if a listed peril damages a neighboring premise and civil authorities prevent the insured from accessing the premise in question.
- Liability & Remedies:
  - Slips and falls on commercial property and casualties caused by snow plows or falling ice could be an issue.
  - Would people sue their town, municipality or utility because of how it handled (or mishandled) the emergency?

- National grid company: a woman filed a petition for a class action lawsuit on behalf of the almost three million people deprived of power during the storm. The utility announced a plan to credit its clients.

1999 – Earthquake – Southern Asia

The event:

- Earthquake of Richter Magnitude 7.7 for 30 seconds
- 10,000 aftershocks (6.5 & 6.8)

Impact:

- Severe damage to buildings non-incorporating seismic design (mostly residential and commercial but not industrial)
- Power Failure (SI) due to city power grid bottleneck impacted by EQ Shock

Consequences:

- The Science Park was impacted by a major power outage due to a single point of failure (a pylon identified after the event) within the power loop supplying the complex. A loop provided more reliability than a dead end or spur arrangement.
- The Science Park was comprised of Semiconductor Fabs occupied for the production of high tech products (ships used in telecom, IT, etc.)
- These semiconductor Fabs were built to a good overall seismic design so that the buildings would withstand such natural perils.
- However, the power outage, greater than the capacity of emergency generators, resulted in the partial contamination of the clean rooms (controlled atmosphere and air filtration needed for the process) and the loss of Work In Progress material inside these rooms, thus, resulting in a loss of revenue under SI..
- Moreover, the breakage of quartz tubes (used in the process) occurred at the same time in several plants as a direct

consequence of the earthquake. This resulted in a Quartz Tube Shortage on the market (lack of spares similar to standard BI).

Example: Gas supplier in Asia Pacific

- Pipeline Explosion in June resulting in interruption of main gas supply in the region reducing Western Australia's supply of energy by up to 35%.
- This resulted in business disruption for utilities (i.e. power stations equipped with Gas Turbines), mining and refining installations (gas fired furnaces) and other petrochemical industries using gas as fuel.
- It also affected other industries such as a petrochemical plant whose feed gas was being used by a Fertilizer Company in its process.
- The Gas Supplier was the sole supplier for the Fertilizer Company. The supply of gas was fully interrupted for almost 3 months before it was partially resumed. Full resumption occurred around 4 months later.
- The Gas Supplier was contractually bound to deliver a certain amount of gas to the Fertilizer Company.
- The Fertilizer Company was buying around USD 600 million CBI / SI combined. The Gas supplier was a named Supplier under the original policy. A claim was sent to the (Re)Insurers.

8. OTHER BI EXTENSION FOCUS

The following so-called "Other BI extensions" may be partially or fully included within the BI, CBI or SI Insurance coverage described in the previous sections. They also may be subject to the "governing perils" and limits previously described. This will depend on the wording.

Just keep in mind that the list is not exhaustive. The imagination of the (Re)Insurance industry seems to have no limits when it comes to including misnomers leading to even more confusion. So, please excuse what is about to follow. Making head or tail of these misnomers is a dirty job but somebody's got to do it.

8.1. Increased Vs Additional Increase in - Cost of Working

The following acronyms and wording may be found:
- ICOW / ICoW / AICOW / AICoW (UK form)
- Extra Expense (US form)
- Extra Cost

These are basically related to the expenditure incurred for each strategic decision taken by the Insured with the intention of mitigating the loss especially in terms of loss of revenue, including but not limited to:
- Subcontracting out some production.
- Renting of alternative factory premises to continue production.
- Renting temporary office accommodation.
- Promotional costs incurred to maintain operations.
- Additional overtime work.
- Costs incurred for accelerating building repairs
- Etc.

Difference between Cost and Expense:
- Business people like to bandy jargon about and these two terms are no exception to the rule.
- They may be used interchangeably in business conversations, but they have different meanings and applications in business.
- First, a general definition of both terms:
  - Cost is "an amount that has to be paid or spent to buy or obtain something. The term "cost" is often used in business in the context of marketing and pricing strategies,
  - The term "expense" implies something more formal and something related to the business balance sheet and taxes.
- For accounting and tax purposes, COSTS are related to business assets and they are shown on the balance sheet. EXPENSES are related to business expenditures over time, and they are shown on the business net income (profit and loss) statement.

Understanding Extra Expense Insurance:
- Extra expense insurance is designed to help a business with any expenses that it might incur while its normal business operations are disrupted. These expenses are often excluded from other types of insurance policies - property insurance, for example - which are designed to help pay for physical damage which results from specific perils. The expenses that are covered under an extra expense insurance policy need to be considered both reasonable and necessary, such as the cost of setting up a temporary office while the damaged office space and equipment is being repaired or replaced.

Difference between Increased Cost of Working and Additional Increase in Cost of Working:

- **Increased Cost of Working (ICOW/ICoW):**
    - This is the additional expenditure necessarily and reasonably incurred for the sole purpose of avoiding or diminishing the reduction in Turnover which, but for that expenditure, would have taken place during the Indemnity Period in consequence of the damage, but not exceeding the sum produced by applying the rate of gross profit to the amount of the reduction thereby avoided.
    - The expense must be for the sole purpose of avoiding or diminishing the reduction in Turnover.

Examples of losses including Increased Cost of Working (ICOW/ICoW):
- Example 1: a pulp and paper mill using air freight for the delivery of critical heavy spares (i.e. economizer for a Black Liquor Recovery Boiler) leading to expensive transportation but limiting turnover to 1 month instead of 4 months had they used marine cargo. The total cost must not exceed the original cost of the loss had marine cargo transportation been used.
- Example 2: major explosion of a unique 60MVA oil filled transformer used in a steel industry. The replacement time was at least 12 months - best case scenario. (Up to 18 months in the worst case including manufacturing and shipping). 12 months BI for the steel mill representing USD 100M. The installation on site would take around one week. The Neighbor, having a spare transformer of the same capacity, proposed to rent the transformer to the steel mill for a global sum of USD 50M until the new transformer was available. This reduction of 50% BI was accepted by the Insurer

- **Additional Increase in Cost of Working (AICOW / AICoW):**
    - The insurance under this item is limited to the increase in cost of working (not otherwise recoverable hereunder) necessarily and reasonably incurred during the Indemnity Period in consequence of the damage for the purpose of

avoiding or diminishing reduction in Turnover and/or resuming and/or maintaining normal business operations and/or services.

- This wider cover allows increased costs that maintain the business or service, but which do not necessarily reduce or avoid a Loss of Turnover during the Indemnity Period.
- For example, an Insured employing additional staff working extra shifts on other process lines or purchasing Finished Products from competitors rebranded as per the Insured Business to ensure (almost) normal sales and services (avoiding loss of market share).
- Typical AICOW/AICoW includes but is not limited to:

  Additional rent for temporary premises

  Outsourcing of manufacture to a competitor or contract manufacturer

  An advertising campaign to win back lost or disgruntled customers

  The hire of temporary plant and/or equipment

  Overtime payment to staff

  The temporary employment of additional staff

- Additional Increase in Cost of Working Cover only: Some Insureds believe that they do not require full business interruption insurance as they will not lose any sales but may incur some additional expenses to maintain sales and customer service. This may be true for some service companies not involving any specialized equipment (i.e. lead time). They claim that they can quickly relocate or have their staff work from home. If this is true then this cover, purchased as a stand-alone cover may be appropriate. This would certainly not be recommended for a manufacturer or retailer. In most cases, it is found that the cover does not adequately indemnify a wholesaler.

Example of a loss including Additional Increase in Cost of Working:
- A fertilizer complex (insured X) is made up of various processing units of which some are Joint ventures (JVs) with overseas investors in order to produce dedicated specialized products for their country.
- Each and every process unit, including those in the JVs, produces steam used for the process (heating source) and for running Steam Turbine Generators producing electric power.
- The generated Steam and Electric Power is mutualized on a Complex Hub consisting of steam pipe and electric feeders so that each and every process unit has sufficient steam and electric power (i.e. availability, reliability, flexibility).
- The surplus electric power generated is sold to the national grid by the Complex Hub. Import of electric power from the national grid is also possible though the Complex Hub.
- There is one Insurance Policy cover (Property Damage and Business Interruption) for the fertilizer complex (insured X) including JVs.
- There is a Service & Utility agreement between the fertilizer complex (insured X) and the JVs for the supply of steam and electric power (internal billing system).
- A fire broke at JV A. It had to stop production for some weeks in January following the disintegration of the unique Steam Turbine Generator.
- Production of JV A resumed partially at the end of January using the steam and electric power supplied from the Complex Hub. Replacement of the damaged Steam Turbine Generator was planned for May (4 months later).
- In the meantime:
    - Electric power had to be purchased from the national grid for supplying JV A.
    - JV A was not able to sell any electric power to the Complex hub (as per Service & Utility agreement). However, JV A sold the steam not used by the Steam Turbine Generator to the Complex Hub.
    - The Complex Hub was not able to sell any surplus electric power to the national grid.

- This led to the following claim:

Description	Cost for Joint Venture A
Repair and maintenance of damaged equipment (PD)	40.000.000
Operating losses Feb-May (BI)	60.000.000
Stop/ lower production on January (BI)	2.000.000
Electric energy purchase from national grid by the complex – Insured X for internal consumption needs of Joint Venture A (not enough electric power at complex) – (similar to ICOW)	25.000.000
Power purchase delivered to Insured X in the framework of Service & Utility agreement (compensating lack of surplus electric power delivered to complex) –- (similar to ICOW)	15.000.000
Shortfall of electrical energy sales	20.000.000
Steam being sold to Insured X	-10.000.000
TOTAL PD & BI (A+B+C)	**152.000.000**

8.2. Alternative Accommodation

Alternative accommodation cover is a part of a policy that comes into play if a property suddenly becomes uninhabitable as a result of an event such as flooding, fire, subsidence or damage caused by a storm.

It means that the policy provider will help find the Insured alternative accommodation and pay costs, so that the Insured is not homeless while the problem is sorted out.

The cover may also provide alternative long-time accommodation of the same standard. This is typically the case for VIP luxury apartments.

Example: A high rise building in Middle East
- The tower building was partially damaged by fire in 2016. External cladding was charred from the 50th floor to the top of the tower.
- Seven days after the fire, 101 apartments were uninhabitable. Their occupants have been offered temporary free lodging by some hotels and houses.
- More than two months after the fire the municipality confirmed no damage to the structure but indicated that 81 units were not habitable.
- All resident owners were covered by insurance for alternative accommodation for up to 3 years.

This cover may be similar to Extra Expense Insurance as described previously but with wider coverage in some cases.

8.3. Loss of Rent

When an Insured is renting a facility to a third party this could result in there being multi-tenant activities on the same site.

The rent is revenue for the Insured. In the case of fire on-site originating at the Insured property also destroying the rented facility, the loss of rent may be added to the Business Interruption of the main site.

8.4. Contingency Extension

Meaning any supply facilities and/or any supply lines (life lines) from which the Insured obtains:
- Electricity, gas, water
- Telecommunications, data services
- Etc.
- Can also include named & un-named suppliers and/or customers
- Limited, sub-limited or not

The above may be assimilated to SI or CBI but may also be proposed only as optional extensions.

8.5. Prevention of Access

Also called:
- "Lack of Egress/Ingress",
- "Denial of Access"
- "Non availability of routes of transport"
- "Port Blockage"

There may be various sorts of access: i.e. harbor, river jetty, roads, rails, etc.

The resulting Business Interruption may involve:

"No Damage" to the Insured property (sometimes called "BI no Damage"):
- The property of the insured may not be accessible from the outside because of the access road being blocked by flood even if there is no Direct Damage to the Insured property.

Damage to the Insured property:
- The single haul road of an 800m deep open cast mine allowing 40tons capacity trucks to handle gold ore can be impaired for several months due to a land slide following heavy rain. In such a case the reinstatement of the haul road may be very expensive and a relatively long business interruption period is expected.

Note that a policy called "Non Damage BI" cover was issued by an insurance company in 2012 after the Thai flood event as a stand-alone policy combining "Non availability of routes of transport" with "Cyber". This cover was purchased by at least one steel maker who was using the nearest river for importing large amounts of feedstock. The main intention was to cover any interruption of business due to extremely high or low river water level conditions preventing barges using the only jetty. This cover was not very successful as the rate was deemed prohibitive (approx. 7 pro mile) and there were many limiting terms and conditions.

Lack of ingress / egress may be related to "Civil authority ingress / egress": Government-mandated closure of business premises that directly causes loss of revenue. Examples include forced business closures because of government-issued curfews or street closures related to a covered event. See next section below.

Example of Port Blockage in Latin America:

- An underwater crude oil pipe linking the refinery onshore to the floating buoy used to transfer crude oil from oil tankers in the harbor was damaged by an anchor.
- Crude oil, lighter than water, was released on the surface of the water in the harbor and was ignited by torch hot work being conducted on a neighboring vessel.
- The surface of the water of the harbor was rapidly engulfed by fire burning for hours.
- The oil tanker promptly escaped out to sea.
- About USD 50M in Property Damage was reported involving 9 fishing boats and severe damage to a fish oil factory located in the harbor.
- The harbor was blocked (no access from sea or land) for 11 days during which time:
    - Finished products could not be exported (e.g. timber, wood planks for Mexico and USA).
    - Crude oil for the refinery could not be imported.
    - Raw material for a pulp mill could not be imported (e.g. wood chips).
- The consequences of this "Port Blockage" were almost not insured.

8.6. Action of Competent Authorities

Also called "Cessation of works by acts of authority (BI).

Authorities Having Jurisdiction (AHJ) are numerous and may have different levels of authority and expertise (i.e. at the level of a county, city, region, country).

Decisions may be taken upon recommendation by a specialized committee. The influence of public opinion may be important.

Actions and decisions of authorities may be based on different considerations such as health, environment, potential social unrest conditions, liability issues, etc.

Actions and decisions of AHJs may be only local or they might extend over a wide territory or airspace (see examples below).

The precautionary principle (or precautionary approach) is a legal approach to innovations or new situations with potential for causing harm when extensive scientific knowledge on the matter is lacking. This is usually the answer to the unknown. The application of the precautionary principle may result in the temporary shutdown of a certain kind of operation in a given country for a relatively long period of time in terms of interruption of business. The notion of time is not the same for administrations as it is for businesses. Some small and medium sized operations may not survive such lengthy mandatory interruptions. Big international organizations are more resilient.

Some insurance cover does exist. However, the extent of cover is limited. Only adequate Risk Management can make the difference which implies having good relationships and a high quality of communication with the AHJ long before any event happens.

Example 1: a pigment manufacture in Scandinavia
- A pigment factory installed along a fjord in Scandinavia was occupied in the crushing and screening of minerals extracted from the nearest quarry to be used as pigment for paints.

- An old tank containing diesel for the emergency generator used for lighting was leaking from the bottom. This was not visible, but it was detected when fishermen reported small amounts of hydrocarbons floating on the surface of the water of the fjord.
- State authorities made the decision to shut down the plant for 6 months for investigations, removal of the tank and decontamination of the ground.
- In the meantime, the plant was not operating.
- The leakage was not due to a sudden and accidental rupture of the tank. This was a gradual contamination due to gradual corrosion. This tank was obviously overlooked in the asset integrity management program (preventive maintenance & inspection).
- Due to the lack of physical loss, the plant could not claim for BI.

Example 2: a fertilizer plant in Continental Europe
- Massive chemical explosion at a fertilizer plant. The impact of the blast wave extended far beyond the fertilizer plant perimeter.
    - Loss: about € 2 billion
    - 75,000 claims
    - 30 casualties and more than 2,000 injured
    - 30,000 homes, 5,000 vehicles, 7,000 professionals hit by the explosion
    - 1 university and 100 schools/high schools
- Moreover, by virtue of an administrative decision, other industries handling hazardous material had to shut down for several weeks as the origin of the loss was not immediately identified.

Example 3: Legionnaires' Disease and cooling tower - Continental Europe
- Symptoms of Legionnaires' disease include coughing, shortness of breath, fever, muscle aches and headaches.

Additional symptoms include diarrhea, nausea, and confusion. Symptoms often appear within 2 to 10 days after exposure but it could take up to 2 weeks for some to experience these symptoms.
- The new case concerned an 80-year-old woman, whose first signs of illness date back to early January. The outbreak, which struck in two waves affected 76 people, 10 of whom died.
- Legionnaires' is often associated with cooling towers and hot tubs as these are areas where bacteria can grow and thrive. These infection hubs also aerosolize water, allowing the bacteria to make its way into the unknowing host quite easily.
- Cooling towers have many industrial uses but the ones that are hot topics for Legionnaires' disease are heating, ventilation, and air conditioning (HVAC) applications.
- If not properly maintained and disinfected, the large amounts of water found in cooling towers are potential breeding grounds for Legionella bacteria. Legionella bacteria are "heat loving bacteria," making the warm temperatures found in cooling towers an ideal home. The nutrients, sediment, heterotrophic biofilm and amoebae contribute to the perfect environment for these bacteria.
- A frozen food processing plant was closed for several weeks following an administrative decision applying the "precautionary principle". This occurred after the discovery at the end of December in an air-cooling tower of Legionella in very small quantities but of a strain already identified in patients.

Example 4: A pulp mill in Latin America
- This new pulp mill was commissioned in 2004 and manufactured paper pulp from the nearest man-made pinewood and eucalyptus forest.
- Declared Total Sum Insured:
    o Property Damage USD 600 million
    o Annual BI: USD 300 million

- This type of occupancy is a big consumer of water needed for the process and taken from the nearest river.

- An effluent treatment plant was installed. All effluents were filtered, neutralized and cooled to a certain temperature in order to preserve the ecosystem prior to being released into the river.

- The plant had to be completely shut down for 34 days shortly after commissioning following an administrative decree pertaining to local environmental regulation concerns.

- After investigation and some changes, which were mostly focused on the water wells, water effluent and environmental contingency plan, the plant was restarted. From a property loss prevention standpoint, these changes affected neither the process operations nor the safety conditions of the plant.

- Moreover, since the plant began operations in 2004 the pulp mill was only operating at 80% of its full design production capacity due to "temporary" governmental restrictions.

- The major leitmotiv of this restriction was that the nameplate design production capacity was higher than the initially forecast design production capacity at the early stage of the project. This may happen when the manufacturer proposes a good deal for equipment with higher capacity and better efficiency before installation.

- However, the pulp mill claimed the fact that the effluent treatment plant was designed with spare capacity able to handle even more effluent than when operating at full nameplate design capacity.

- In 2008, the pulp mill was still waiting for administrative clearance to operate at full design nameplate capacity.

Example 5 : 2010 Europe Air Travel Disruption

- The 2010 eruption of a volcano was a sequence of volcanic events in an island of the North Atlantic known for relatively minor volcanic eruptions.

- Seismic activity started at the end of 2009 and gradually increased in intensity until March 2010, a small eruption occurred that was rated 1 out of 8 (worst case) on the volcanic Explosivity scale.
- By mid-April 2010, the eruption entered a second phase and created an ash cloud.
- This eruption caused enormous **disruption to air travel** across Western and Northern Europe **over an initial period of 6 day**.
- Additional localized disruptions continued into May 2010
- Consequently, a very high proportion of flights within, to, and from Europe were cancelled creating the **highest level of air travel disruption since the Second World War**.
  - 100,000 flights cancelled
  - More than 10 million passengers stacked
  - Between € 1.5 and 2.5 billion loss in Europe for travel agents, airlines and tourism organizations.
  - No insurance coverage
- Other consequences - 2010 eruptions:
  - Evacuation of about 500 farmers and their families from areas in in this island in the North Atlantic
  - Short and long-term weather and environmental effects (suspicion of fluoride poisoning of livestock)
  - Impact on economy (Service Interruption)
  - Impact on cultural events in Northern Europe
- From a Risk Management Standpoint:
  - This was a Non-identified risk - Non foreseen situation (first air travel disruption of such amplitude).
- Decision of Authorities Having Jurisdiction (AHJ):
  - Aircraft manufacturers indicated that planes should avoid any contact with volcanic particles - in June 24 1982, an aircraft (B747-British airways) flew into a cloud of volcanic

ash thrown up by the eruption of Mount Galunggung in Indonesia resulting in the failure of all four engines. The reason for the failure was not immediately apparent to the crew or ground control. The aircraft was diverted to Jakarta in the hope that enough engines could be restarted to allow it to land there. The aircraft was able to glide far enough to exit the ash cloud, and all engines were restarted (although one failed again soon after), allowing the aircraft to land safely.
  - Based on the above, aviation authorities applied the principle of precaution resulting in air space closure.
- European Airlines – Crisis Management Plan:
  - Organizing « experimental » flights in Europe and analyzing potential effects on planes including engines
  - Submitting results to aviation authorities
- Flight clearance was obtained from aviation authorities by the end of April, 2010

Example 6: Tailing Dams in Latin America
- Residue from mining and ore processing operations are usually stored in a tailing dam. Many large mining entities have a long legacy of tailings dams which, in some cases, have been used for decades.
- These tailing dams are basically multi-component special hazards. This is not just a big stack of dry material. The content of some dams can reach millions of cubic meters of water. Dewatering, stability supervision and movement monitoring is therefore key especially when considering life exposure and safety issues (i.e. villages built downstream).
- In 2019 a dam decommissioned in 2015 collapsed. This was the mining company's second dam in this country to fail in just over three years.
- Further to these two events local authorities announced that all operations involving tailing dams across the country should shut down until they could prove that the dams were safe. Providing extensive information about dams installed and even

decommissioned some decades ago is not easy. In some cases, due to lack of documentation, "as if studies" are conducted. In the above case it all took some months during which time the related mining and ore processing operations were shut down.
- Without any physical damage at their property these mining operations could not claim for any BI compensation as per Property policy cover and BI extension. This was a net loss for the Organizations.
- Note that even in the case of physical damage resulting in BI due to administrative closure of the operations, the indemnity is usually sub limited.

8.7. Loss of Attraction

Loss of Attraction is an extension to business interruption insurance protecting the policyholder against a reduction in turnover as a result of an insured event somewhere in the vicinity that reduces the trade of the insured.

The above definition seems very similar to the definition of the "CBI Leader Property" (section 6.4.3).

Example: 2005 Hurricane - beach resorts area in Central America
- The Hurricane sustained winds of 150mph and gusts up to 184mph.
- The Hurricane directly hit a famous beach resort area in Central America causing severe damage.
- The Hurricane was the most powerful hurricane ever recorded and completely decimated the tourist industry for around 6 months in this area.
- Many hotels were damaged, some beyond repair. Shops, bars and restaurants suffered flooding and structural damage. Downtown infrastructure was decimated, with power lines down and residents without electricity or water for over a week in some cases.
- Other hotels were built to standards destined to resist such natural perils.

- The resilience and determination of the local people, together with the unprecedented support from their Government, ensured that this beach area recovered and was even better than before.
- Once infrastructures including utilities were restored some hotels could have re-opened.
- However, the public beaches were severely damaged by the Hurricane. The sand was removed revealing dangerous shallow rocks on the surface.
- A huge beach recovery program took place restoring the beaches to a condition better than before Hurricane hit.
- However, it took several months. The loss of revenue for some hotels not suffering any direct damage from the Hurricane was assimilated as "Loss of Attraction" by them due to the public beaches being impaired. These beaches were what attracted their customers.

8.8. "CBI No Damage"

The term « CBI No Damage" is typically a case of a misnomer or mislabeling of an insurance cover.

This, moreover, does not refer to a stand-alone CBI.

Let's have a look at the following example:

Examples 1: "CBI No Damage" used sometimes in the southern part of Africa

© Franck Orset (FPO)

- A shark attack occurred on a Wednesday off the coast. The attack was reported on TV news showing the hotel nearby. All bookings were consequently cancelled, thus generating a loss of revenue (loss of customers and no damages).
- Note that the same result may be obtained with a guest committing suicide in a room of the same hotel when reported on TV-news.

A gentleman from the local insurance market told me that the origin of the name given to this cover (CBI No Damage) is not clearly established. It may have appeared at a time when the country suffered a power outage due to high demand exceeding the capacity of the grid. Property damages such as spoiled food and the loss of revenue due to utility failure may have been called "CBI No Damage". This introduces even more confusion as it is very similar to "Service Interruption" (see section 7).

The term "CBI No damages" is also found in Northern Europe designating, as in the southern part of Africa, "Loss of attraction".

8.9. Potpourri

Based on the above it is easy to understand that the name of a given Insurance cover may have a different meaning all over the world. Let's end this section with a selection of those acronyms, names of cover and summary of extent of coverage:

- "CBI" / "Supply chain multi cases" / "NDBI (Non Damage BI)". This basically may cover or may not cover (even exclude) one or more of the following cases:
  - Bankruptcy, strike,
  - denial of access,
  - port blockage,
  - cyber attack,
  - decision of authorities,
  - political sanctions,
  - pandemics,
  - communicable diseases / infectious diseases

Definitions and wordings should be crystal clear in each case so that all parties involved have a clear understanding of what they are talking about.

9. OTHER BI RELATED CONSEQUENCES

9.1. Induced Financial Consequences following a loss

As a matter of fact, the (Re)Insurance industry is often mistaken for "Santa Claus":

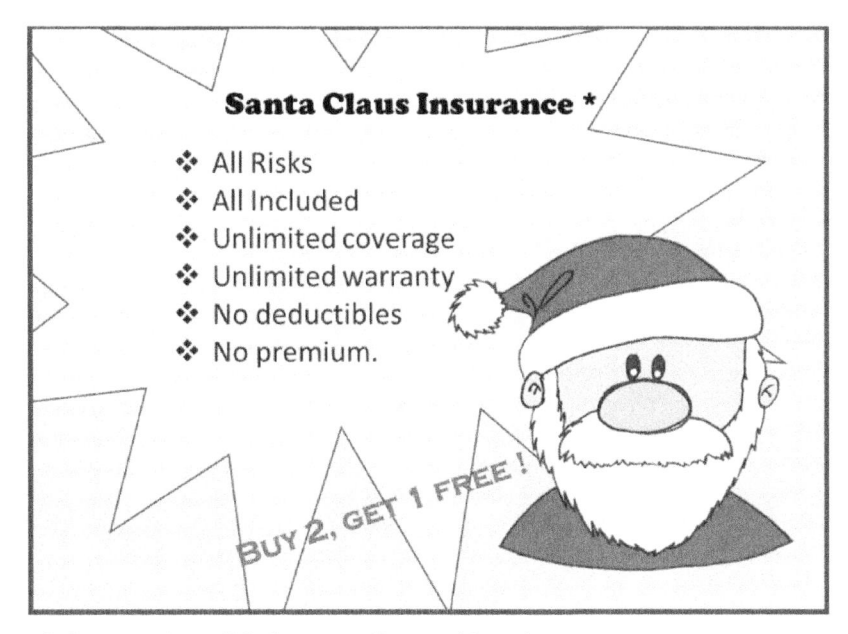

Santa Claus Insurance *
- All Risks
- All Included
- Unlimited coverage
- Unlimited warranty
- No deductibles
- No premium.

BUY 2, GET 1 FREE!

* *Do people still believe in Santa Claus?*
© Franck Orset (FPO)

The role of the (Re)Insurance industry is to help support the economy. This support cannot exceed the capacity of the (Re)Insurer. There are, therefore, some limits defined in a contract before any loss occurs.

At the end of the year, just after Christmas, an insured cannot claim for the reimbursement of the premium he paid 12 months before if his business has not suffered any loss that year. In much the same way you cannot claim for the reimbursement of your health care insurance premium because you did not undergo prostate surgery during the year.

133

Let's be serious, we all want A-rated, well-financed, sustainable (Re)Insurers. Risks should at least be paid out to the carrier.

Moreover, the consequences of a financial loss for an organization may extend far beyond the indemnity paid by the (Re)Insurance.

There may also be no (Re)Insurance solution available for some events having unlimited consequences (i.e. not limited to a financial loss in monetary terms). Some of these events are called "systemic risks" that may impact the global economy of a country, region, continent or even the entire planet such as:
- Africa 2014: Ebola virus (< USD 800 billion)
- USA/Europe 2017: WannaCry/NotPetya (> USD 2 billion)
- France 2019: civil unrests, Yellow Jackets (> USD 1 billion)
- Chile 2019: civil unrests (USD 4 billion PDBI / NDBI?)
- USA 2019: withdrawal of FDA certification (USD X billion)
- Worldwide 2020: Covid-19 pandemic (To Be Defined)

9.2. Loss of market Share

The loss of market share after a loss is typically an induced financial consequence for which there is no obvious (Reinsurance) solution so far.

Example: A Cardboard Factory in Latin America
- This cardboard factory was specialized in the production of cardboard trays for the exporting of fresh fruit, fish and frozen fish from Latin America to the entire world.
- This is typically a mass production business. The margin is relatively low. Flexibility is key for adapting the production line to the client's need (i.e. format, printing). Basically, they work on order and there is a strong seasonal impact. It is usual to work with extra shifts which require additional manpower. The Cardboard Factory is made of sandwich panels with highly combustible plastic insulation. There is no automatic fire protection.
- During the night a fire broke out and destroyed the Cardboard Factory.

- It took 12 months to rebuild the Cardboard Factory incorporating non-combustible construction material, automatic fire protection and the latest, more efficient production equipment.
- Most of the property loss was paid by the Property Insurance program except for betterment. The BI extension included an indemnity for the loss of revenue for 12 months which covered the reinstatement period.
- However, in the meantime, the customers of the Cardboard Factory plant found new cardboard manufacturers who stole them away with good offers.
- It took 5 years after the Cardboard Factory was rebuilt to recover the same level of sales. This involved advertising the brand and looking for new markets (i.e. additional costs for the insured).

9.3. Loss of Reputation

The reputation of an Organization is definitely a valuable intangible asset

Loss of reputation may be far more destructive than any physical loss for almost any Organization. It can happen because of a physical event but that is not always the case as shown in the following examples. So far, there is no suitable (Re)Insurance solution.

Example: an International Food Group

- An environmental organization posted a movie on social media accusing the International Food Group of using palm oil, thus contributing to de-forestation in Indonesia and to the extinction of the Orangutan.
- The International Food Group was forced to drop some of its palm oil suppliers.

Example: an audit & consulting firm in Northern America

- This firm was created in 1932 (specialized in accounting)
- In 1950's their expertise extended to legal, taxes, etc.
- 1959 expansion in Europe
- 1979 became the world leader in their field of expertise
- 2001: USD 9.3 billion revenue, 85 000 employees, 390 offices within 94 Countries
- At the end of 2001: a scandal revealed a conflict of interest with this firm and an energy company (audited by the firm since 1986)
- In 2002 the firm had lost all major clients (lack of confidence)
- Most of the business just disappeared since competitors showed no interest in any salvage (reputational risk).

Example: 1990' Sparkling Water Company Western Europe

- This family-owned company had produced sparkling mineral water since 1900'.
- In 1980' the Sparkling Water company was selling about 300 million bottles in North America representing 80 % of all imported water.
- In 1990 a very low concentration of benzene (fossil origin) was discovered by a Northern American lab in 13 bottles (reportedly due to human error: a filter was not replaced on time). No risk for humans was reported.
- The Sparkling Water Company decided to recall 280 million bottles from 6 countries. (i.e. € 150 Million loss). The company's reputation was hit resulting in a considerable loss of sales which, in turn, rendered the company financially fragile.
- In 1992 an International Food Company took over the Sparkling Water Company (€ 1.2 billion investment reported).

9.4. Other

Other consequences of a loss on an Organization may include but are not limited to:

- Reduced PD/BI/CBI/SI Insurance coverage capacity (the insurance market becoming risk adverse).
- Reduced Credit capabilities (the banks are reluctant having lost confidence).
- Reluctant Investors (loss of confidence).
- Cash flow issue (suppliers still need to be paid even when the loss has occurred).

This list is not exhaustive.

10. BUSINESS INTERRUPTION & CONTINGENT BI MITIGATION

10.1. Breaking the Myth of Confidence

"People hate to think about bad things happening, so they always underestimate their likelihood."
&
"Time is a variable continuum."

— Michael Lewis, The Big Short: Inside the Doomsday Machine

The terrorist attacks of September 11, 2001 dramatically increased the awareness of threat sources and vulnerabilities for nearly all organizations.

However, it is surprising that so many businesses are still unprepared today for Business Interruption.

According to some studies made on small and medium sized businesses:

- About 50% of the relatively big organizations that have suffered a major loss disappear within the next 2 years.
- Around 40% of medium sized businesses fail within 5 years of surviving a major Business Interruption incident.
- Businesses that take more than 30 days to get back to normal operations are "highly likely" to go out of business.

The total impact of a Business Interruption incident may be underestimated. The scope of continuity planning in Organizations is usually limited by the magnitude and timescale of the Incident:

- Magnitude of Incident Impact: large scale disasters are imagined to be too costly or too big for the business to deal with (this is "Somebody Else's Problem")

- Timescale of incident: short term problems such as staff absenteeism are regarded as "everyday occurrences' not worthy of preparing for, whilst long-term issues such as management development are considered non-urgent and are therefore set aside ("Lost in Translation").

The attitude above results in a "comfort zone" of issues considered as manageable, but which fails to address the full range of the continuity threat. Potential threats or problems that fall outside the comfort zone are simply not considered an important enough investment of time and effort.

The Disaster Recovery Plan or Business Continuity Plan does not usually consider that the worst can happen. Murphy's Law is just ignored (e.g. "things will go wrong in any given situation, if you give them a chance").

© Franck Orset (FPO)

Most organizations even confuse the Business Continuity Plan with the Emergency Response that limits the loss so that it won't impact the continuity of their business.

According to their scenarios, the fire fighters risking their life in case of a major fire at the Organization are playing the role of Risk Managers ensuring property conservation and business continuity. If that were the case, the fire fighters at least deserve a medal and there is no longer any need for insurance.

But keep in mind that "blindness to our own weaknesses is why overconfidence is a silent killer".

In order for an organization to have a chance of surviving after a maybe-remote-but-still possible major event there is no need to reinvent the wheel. The well-known principles of modern Risk Management apply. A complete review of all operations should be conducted in accordance with this global approach of the risk as summarized below.

Usual Risk Management Diagram, the so called Risk Management "Virtuous circle":

1. Risk Analysis:
   a. Identification
   b. Assessment   (Risk Mapping)

3. Communication:
   Internal
   External

2. Risk Response:
   a. Risk Control
   b. Risk Financing

4. Risk Auditing:
   Inspection & review

© Didier Schütz (DLS)

1. **Risk Analysis**: identify all "Events" that may impact any entities (so called "Risk Object") of the organization and assess the impact at the level of the entity itself but also for the Organization. The combination of "Event" and "Risk Object" is commonly called a "Vulnerability". The assessment basically consists in quantifying what can be quantified and adopting a qualitative approach when necessary (i.e. reputational risk). The result of the risk analysis usually leads to the "Risk Mapping" (Severity / Probability curve). Step 1 is just an inventory of the risk. Risk Mapping is not the final goal. It is just a tool for defining the rest of the journey.

2. **Risk Response**: there are different levels of vulnerabilities spotted on a Risk Map. Most vulnerabilities can be addressed locally by Management in coordination with the Risk

Management of the group. Some other vulnerabilities maybe be beyond the scope of local management requiring strong support at corporate level. This is typically the case when speaking about supply chains involving interactions inside the Organization and outside with customers and suppliers. The Risk Response consists of two steps:

a. **Risk Control**: term given to any measures for preventing the occurrence of an event when possible, any protection measure for mitigating the impact of an event when impacting the Organization, and finally a Contingency Plan and or a Business Continuity Plan for giving all possible chances of suitable recovery to an Organization in case prevention and protection measures are not sufficient or even not possible in some cases.

b. **Risk Financing**: the residual risk that cannot be fully addressed by the Risk Control above is "transferred" to a third party wanting and having the capacity of financing the risk such as the (Re)Insurance market. The risk transfer can also consist of other options when possible such as a retention by the Organization (self-financing through a reserve) or a line of credit signed in advance (*) or Alternative Risk Transfer solutions – ART (**).

Notes:
(*) Line of credit: This is a credit facility extended by a bank or other financial institution to a business when it needs funds. A line of credit takes several forms, such as an overdraft limit, demand loan, special purpose, etc. It is effectively a source of funds that can readily be tapped at the borrower's discretion. Interest is paid only on money actually withdrawn. Lines of credit can be secured by collateral, or may be unsecured.)

(**) The ART market is a portion of the insurance market that allows companies to purchase coverage and transfer risk without having to use traditional commercial insurance. Thus, it includes:

Insurance-linked Notes (ILN): typically referred to as "catastrophe-linked bonds" or simply "CAT bonds". CAT bonds are risk-linked securities that transfer a specified set of risks from a sponsor to investors. They were created and first used in the mid-1990s in the aftermath of Hurricane Andrew and the Northridge earthquake. CAT bonds are designed to protect companies from events like massive hurricanes and earthquakes, which happen rarely but cause enormous damage. The bonds pay interest and return principal the way other debt securities do - as long as a catastrophe that causes losses above an agreed-upon limit doesn't whack the issuer.

Captives and Mutuals: Captive insurance is an alternative to self-insurance in which a parent group or groups create a licensed insurance company to provide coverage for itself. A parent company, trade association, or a group of companies within an industry can set up a captive insurance company. These entities can be used for financing the retention risk as well as risk transfer.

Finite Insurance: Unlike most reinsurance contracts, finite risk contracts are usually multiyear. In other words, they spread risk over time and generally take into account the investment income generated over the period. An Organization seeking protection makes a large premium to an insurer, the amount being sufficient to cover the insurer's expected losses. The premium is then held by an insurer in an interest-bearing account. If at the end of the policy's term the actual losses are less than the premium, the insurer pays the difference to the corporation. However, if the losses exceed the premium, the corporation makes an additional premium payment to the insurer for the difference.

Multiline Insurance: offers a tool for better integrated risk management by offering one large aggregate limit across several lines of business such as liability, property, and business interruption. The insurer makes a payment if the combined losses on all lines reach a specified amount. The programs usually operate on a multiyear basis. The corporation deals with only one insurer rather than several insurers covering different lines.

Contingent Insurance: often referred to as "contingent cover", is an option granted by an insurance company giving a corporation the right to enter into an insurance contract at some future date. All of the terms of the insurance contract that can be entered into, including the premium that must be paid if the option is exercised, are specified at the time the contingent cover policy is purchased by the corporation.

Swap: This is an agreement between two counterparties to exchange financial instruments or cashflows or payments for a certain time. The instruments can be almost anything but most swaps involve cash based on a notional principal amount.

3. **Communication**: The pre-requisite condition for a Risk Management program to be efficient is the full commitment of all stakeholders of the Organization. The establishment of such a program usually involves a deep cultural change in mindsets at each and every level. All employees become a "Risk Manager" exchanging with the "Risk Manager Coordinator" at corporate level. The program should be understood by everybody. Adequate communication is key at this stage, both internally but also externally, since a good Risk Management program enhances an Organization's credit in many respects (e.g. resilience, sustainability, governance) which, in turn, is greatly appreciated by the business partners including (Re)Insurance.

4. **Risk Auditing:** depending on the type of business a given Organization may change rapidly over a relatively short period of time, absorbing new subsidiaries, developing new products, acquiring new markets in different countries. All this will give rise to new vulnerabilities. The Risk Response defined in step 3 above may rapidly be obsolete and need to be upgraded, starting over back at step 1. The frequency of reviews should be defined by the Organization itself as they, after all, are the ones with the knowledge required. It's basically a never ending process.

All of the above has been clearly defined and detailed in multiple books. Recognized educational programs include the 'Associate in Risk Management' – ARM. An associate in risk management designation is a nationally recognized educational program for dedicated risk management professionals, developed by the Insurance Institute of America.

When speaking of supply chain and potential business interruption, the above Risk Management program should be rolled out without overlooking any of the steps. This includes understanding the interaction between the different entities of an Organization on the one hand and between the organization and its various business partners on the other.

10.2. Understanding the Interactions

It is vital to have an updated process flow chart showing the flow of Raw Material, Work In Progress and Finished Products between the entities of the Organization and the business partners.

You may find the above statement pretty obvious but, believe it or not, some organizations grow so fast, getting bigger and bigger, that the process flow becomes somewhat blurred. Some Organizations even send their semi-Finished Products to be processed by a third party before it is finally customized in one of their own operations. Imagine how complex it can become!

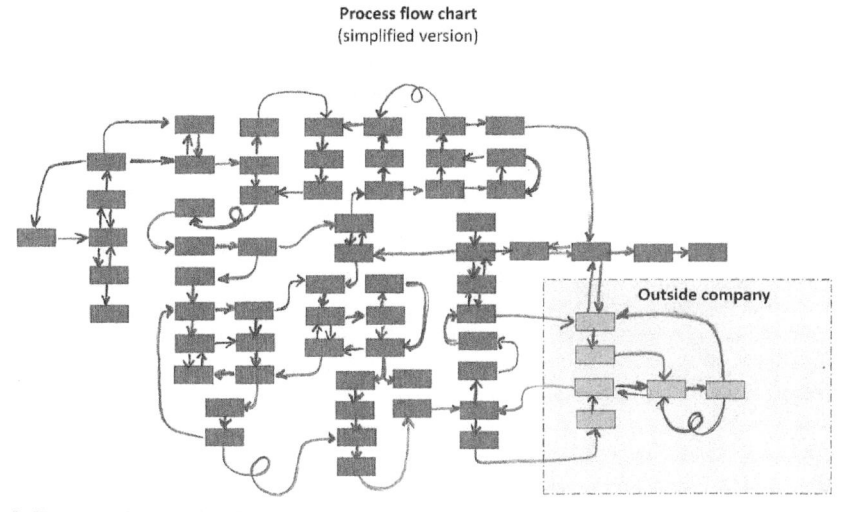

Process flow chart
(simplified version)

© Franck Orset (FPO)

Establishing the list of suppliers and customers may be a challenge. Suppliers may change several times a year depending on market price, demand and offer.

Some organizations may look for the cheapest Raw Material and do not hesitate switching to a new supplier regardless of potential quality of material or logistical issues.

Or they want to be dependent on one sole supplier for cost reduction purposes. Some Organizations do not hesitate to literally depend on one major customer only, representing more than 60% of their sales, while others prefer to diversify.

Once we have a list of suppliers and customers (and the process flow) it is time to do the "Supply Chain Mapping", showing all internal and external interactions.

The best graphic representation I have seen so far is the so-called "Isoproba diagram" showing:

- All interactions between either proper entities or suppliers and customers.
- The level of each and every entity, supplier and customer within the supply chain (i.e. Tier) and the type.
- The potential perils one or more locations could be exposed to depending on their geographic situation. Some software can be used for simulations.

Example of an "Isoproba" diagram showing all interactions and tier levels (basically the supply chain):

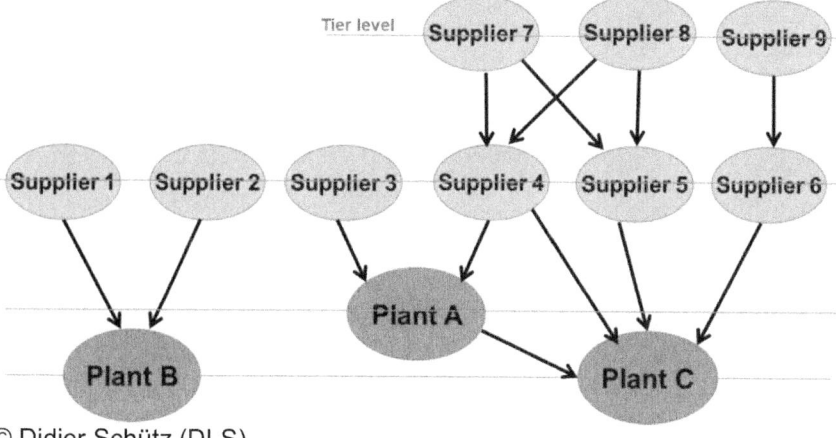

© Didier Schütz (DLS)

Example of a simulation based on the diagram above grouping suppliers in a scenario of events per geographical area:

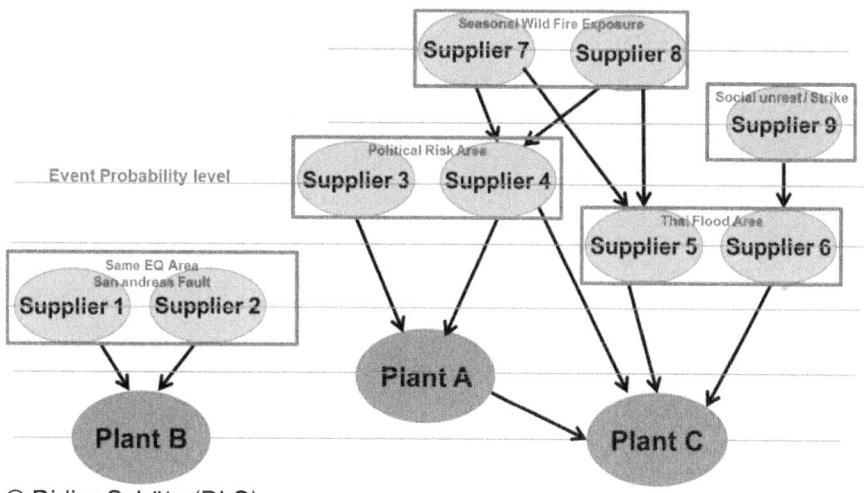

© Didier Schütz (DLS)

However, remember that this diagram is not magic. A lot of systems available on the market are very promising. The most important thing is to have reliable data entered into the tool first. Garbage in – Garbage out should be the rule of thumb here. Not having any reliable data is a little bit like having a Ferrari in a country where they only have regularly flooded unpaved roads.

A BI/CBI exposure analysis may mobilize a lot of specialized resources for reviewing and/or establishing:
- Upstream Origin / Sourcing of Raw Material / Components.
- Dependencies on Suppliers & Potential Alternatives.
- Replacement Time of machinery & availability of Spares.
- Potential dependency upon computerized control systems.
- Internal Organization - Sister Plants Interdependencies.
- Downstream (internal) Exposures - Identification of bottlenecks in the manufacturing process.
- Identification of possible BI/CBI consequences of a shutdown following all possible scenarios (including Property Loss but not limited to).
- Existence of a Contingency plan (CP - formalized & well documented) which would assess:
  o Loss of suppliers.
  o Alternative supply sources.
  o Prioritize assembly lines.
  o Alternative assembly capabilities.

Warning: there are some limitations as to what a "Supply Chain Map" can deliver even when modelized by the best tool of the moment sold by the most famous and fashionable Risk Management guru of the year.

Counting the numbers and tiers of suppliers in a supply chain in a fast-changing, highly-connected world could be an exercise in futility.

It's better to focus limited resources on identifying key value chains in the organization i.e. those production chains where key customers / key products / key margins are involved and the most significant contributions to corporate value are generated.

This is the triage that should be undertaken as a priority. Key supplier / customer dependencies must be identified and assessed for their business interruption impact.

10.3. Establishing a Resilience Strategy

10.3.1. Favorite Weapons (CP, BCP/M)

The « favorite weapons » for step 2 of the "Risk Response" of the Risk Managements' virtuous circle are:
- Contingency Plan (CP)
- Business Contingency Plan

There is usually much confusion regarding terminology used when it is about Contingency Plan, Business Continuity Plan (BCP) / Management (BCM) or even Disaster Recovery Plan. Giving a standard definition would be very difficult since almost all industry sectors have their own. The two most common definitions are given below for information:

- **Contingency Plan (CP):** The purpose of a CP is to mitigate the consequences of a potential loss in terms of business interruption in case of loss of a critical utility or machinery /equipment or sub process unit. This contingency plan should be established, taking all the critical facilities into consideration, such as process machinery & equipment, electrical rooms, transformers, lubrication oil group. This is particularly suitable for self-sufficient sites located in remote locations.
  - All critical facilities, machinery and equipment should be identified.
  - The availability of all critical spare parts should be defined. Critical spares with a relatively long lead time should be available on-site.
  - Machinery and equipment representing severe bottlenecks should be duplicated and stored or installed in separate fire areas.
  - In the case where duplication and/or separation are impossible, adequate protection should be installed.

- **Business Continuity Plan (BCP):** The BCP goes beyond the usual contingency or recovery plans. An organized BCP requires a continuous risk review top-down or bottom-up with the full support and commitment of top management as resources have to be assigned, aligned or re-aligned, such as the case may be. Business interruption could be related to an earthquake, a severe storm, a fire, power outage over a wide area or the complete inaccessibility of a facility for an extended period of time. It should be clear that the cause of the interruption is not important. What is most important is Management's ability to acquire control of the interruption. This is particularly suitable for sites with multiple interdependencies between sister plants and or highly dependent from suppliers / customers.

- Within a BCP, the above existing Contingency Plan should be extended to a scenario-based major disaster, such as the total loss of one processing unit or an event impacting several plants in a relatively wide area (e.g. Earthquake, Hurricane).
- The possibility of the partial recovery of the activity, inside and outside the group, should be investigated.
- The potential interdependencies with the sister plants, upstream and downstream, should be seriously considered.

Notes:
- Business Continuity Management – BCM – is also used instead of CP and or BCP.
- Disaster Recovery Plan was originally used for IT systems but is widely used now.

At the end of the day, the main purpose of these mitigating measures is to ensure Management's ability to acquire control of the interruption.

In order to prevent any confusion in this document BCP is used at the level of a group when one single event can impact different plants/entities (holistic view). The term CP is used at the level of a given plant/entity (site view).

10.3.2. Reliability Issue (CP, BCP/M)

As a matter of fact, it is extremely difficult, if not virtually impossible, to make a CP, BCM/P utterly fool proof or fail safe, meeting all the following criteria, considering that conditions may change over time (i.e. management, organization, priorities, etc.):

- Consider all possible scenarios
- Avoid over-estimated back-up (CP) and/or resilience (BCP) capabilities
- Implement formalized documentation
- Organize regular testing
- Review, update, upgrade documents when needed
- Ensure clear leadership (who is responsible for what & when?)

As a result of the above CP and BCP/M are:

- Often designed as a posteriori disaster Supply Kit.
- Expecting that everything can be done "by the book".
- Not always expecting the unexpected.
- Not always ensuring that companies can easily adjust to major shifts in markets or operating conditions

10.3.3. When to consider a CP as reliable

Regarding the Contingency Plan (CP) as per the definition given above (i.e. loss of a critical utility, machinery, sub process unit), a CP can be considered as reliable when it is about duplication and to some extent about redundancy and spare capacity as detailed below.

- **Duplication:** two sub units are duplicated so that in case of the loss of one unit there will be no critical disruption in the process. This could consist of:
  - Two operating sub-units (so called hot site in IT), such as two PLC servers or two independent substations feeding the site on a loop.
  - Two sub-units of which on duty and one on standby (so called cold site in IT), the standby unit taking over in case of failure of the usual unit on duty. This could take some

time in the case of a manual transfer and/or synchronization needed (e.g. for a power generating unit reaching full load or national grid connection using an Automatic Transfer Switch - ATS).
- o Note that for reliability the duplicated units should be well separated and segregated at least from a fire and explosion standpoint and also from a natural perils and exposure standpoint when possible (e.g. flood). A potential single failure point upstream or downstream of the duplicated units should be clearly identified and eliminated.

- **Redundancy:** the way to express the redundancy level has evolved within recent years as follows:
  - o Up till recently: N+1 meant that N units on duty are able to run normal operations and that there is one more unit available.
  - o Today: N-1 is used instead of N+1. This means that even with one unit out of order operations are still normal.
  - o The above N+1 and N-1 (e.g. transformers) means the same: there is one more online unit available that could take over in case of failure of one unit on duty.
  - o Note that the main purpose of N+1 / N-1 redundancy is for maintenance: one unit can be put offline for maintenance and replaced by the N+1 unit.
  - o Note that maintenance may include a major overhaul or refurbishment of one unit. This could take several months in some cases if it includes dismantling and shipping overseas (e.g. ST/GT major rotor overhaul, transformers).
  - o Based on the above, in the case of the loss of one operating unit while the other unit is offline for maintenance, the related process unit may have to reduce production or even shut down.
  - o As a result, reliable redundancy should include N+2 /N-2 units: one standby unit allowing for maintenance and one more unit providing full back up for one unit.
  - o Note that for reliability all units should be physically well separated and segregated at least from a fire and explosion standpoint (e.g. transformers separated by blast

walls) and also from a natural perils and exposure standpoint when possible (e.g. flood).

- **Spare capacity:** some units may have spare capacity compared to standard operating demand. For example: two transformers needed for feeding a plant. Both transformers have a 50% capacity each so that in the case of failure of one transformer the other could at least provide 75% of the standard operating demand. This spare capacity may be considered as reliable for the Contingency Plan under the following conditions:
  - Two units having spare capacity and physically connected so that one unit could provide partial back up in reasonable time without generating a major disruption. In the case of an automatic load shedding sequence being initiated preventing the single operating transformer from overloading because of the failure of the other unit, the restoration of the electrical power source may take a while depending on the complexity of the power distribution systems.
  - All units should be physically well separated and segregated at least from a fire and explosion standpoint avoiding mutual exposure in case of fire / explosion and also from a natural perils and exposure standpoint when possible (e.g. flood).
  - A potential single failure point upstream or downstream of the duplicated units should be clearly identified and eliminated (e.g. one single power feeding the two transformers).

Other Contingency Plans may include:
- A contract with a supplier or a manufacturer for the replacement of a unit within a reasonable timeframe. This should be signed in advance ensuring that the spares are promptly available at the supplier's / manufacturer's site.
- A back up provided by a sister plant mutualizing spares at group level for all plants. For example, a spare rotor for steam turbines. However, the plants may have turbines from different manufacturers (e.g. Siemens, GE, former ABB, Alstom). In such cases a spare rotor should be available for each and

every type of turbine. The storage and maintenance conditions of the spares are really important. For example, the spare rotor of a turbine should be protected against corrosion using special coating and wrapping or even stored vertically in a nitrogen atmosphere in order to prevent any metal stress. Non-adequate storage conditions and maintenance of spares could lead to a major failure when installed and operated. The obsolescence of some equipment should also be considered. The spares may not be available anymore.

- A back up provided by a competitor or a neighbor having the same equipment and/or a spare on his site. This could be based on mutual agreement or upon a renting contract. When not agreed in advance the cost of rent may be very high, hiked up by the owner taking advantage of the no-choice situation of the plant suffering the loss.
- Logistics such as transportation of the spares should be organized in advance when needed. Special large vehicles and authorization from the Authority Having Jurisdiction may be needed. Transportation by air cargo operated by few specialized companies may be required.
- Other constraints such as customs clearance should be anticipated.

The reliability of the above CPs may be questionable especially on a long term basis considering all above-mentioned criteria and key parameters.

Example: the "almost" Contingency Plan of an underground gold mine

- The underground mine is located in the Northern Hemisphere and exposed to extreme sub-freezing temperatures during winter time.
- The underground mine is 1,000m deep using two shafts: one for ventilation and one for material and transporting the men.
- The hoist for material and men is one of the most critical components consisting of a 1,000m steel rope attached to a drum driven by an electric driver fed from two transformers providing mutual back up connected to the grid.
- The drum is the most critical spare part consisting of 8 sections of several tons each that must be assembled - 9 months minimum replacement time reported.

- According to the insured, there was reportedly a spare hoist and auxiliary equipment that was kept somewhere in a location adjacent to the insured's facility. This hoist was planned to be used for parts if needed. According to the mine's management the switchover wouldn't take too long.
- However, we had a couple of concerns when going on-site for our annual loss prevention inspection:
  - First: how was this hoist stored? (given the environment it was highly likely there could be potential metal degradation and oxidation). Second: gears and bearings also needed to be properly stored
  - Third: when had the last major inspection of the hoist been done and, if it had been done, were any cracks or other types of deficiencies found and what types of corrective measures were taken?
- We asked to visit the facility where the spare drums and auxiliaries were supposed to be stored. The mine management was very transparent and cooperative and took us to an old airfield used at the time of mining prospection 70 years ago. The spare drum parts and auxiliaries were stored in a paved area that was the remains of a hangar made of light bar joists covered with the remains of a tarpaulin regularly buffeted by storms. All spares showed evidence of corrosion. Suddenly switching with the operating drum when needed did not appear quite so easy. The spare had obviously just been forgotten.
- The mine management, fully understanding what Risk Management entailed, took immediate action for inspecting, maintaining and storing these valuable assets considered as critical. Moreover, a pre-planning procedure was written so that the switch in case of failure would be as safe and efficient as possible. This included manpower, tools, transport, work permits needed, possible adverse weather conditions, etc.

10.3.4. CP, BCP/M for Supply Chain

The establishment of a Contingency Plan (CP) or Business Contingency Plan for securing a supply chain may appear very expensive when you consider that it is all about a foreseeable, possible, probable loss that has not yet occurred and/or (what is even worse) might never have occurred in the history of mankind (e.g. WTC prior 9/11 2001).

The losses usually reported within the industrial and commercial sector have a relatively low probability as they are too infrequent to be included in statistical figures.

As far as commercial and industrial risks are concerned, few statistics and reports are, in fact, available. The statistical population is not representative. Motor and life insurance are much better equipped for a pure statistical approach.

As a result of the above, the decision for developing a CP, BCP/M for a given business should be based on Cost Vs Benefit in the case of a loss rather than based on probability for which there is no reliable figure.

Cost Versus Benefit: the benefit of a having a reliable BCP is the difference in cost for recovering from a major loss with a BCP and without a BCP:

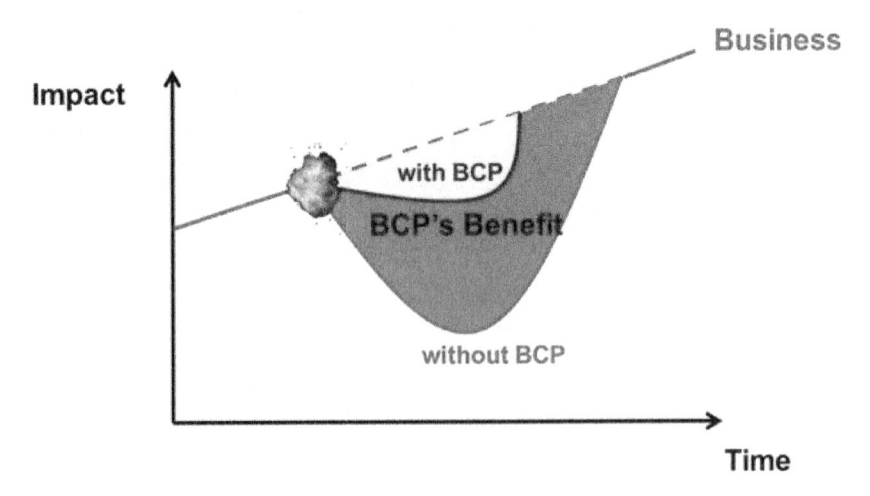

© Didier Schütz (DLS)

With a CP/ BCP: As mentioned above, the key to success is anticipation. Improvisation, when the loss is occurring or after the fact, may cost the Organization much more and may not be very efficient at all. Anticipation is key to ensuring an efficient leverage effect:

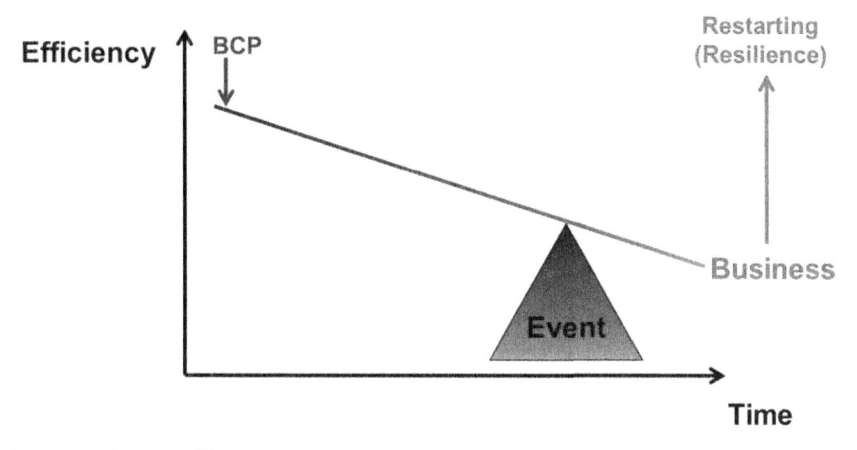

Efficiency ↑ BCP ↓ ... Restarting (Resilience) ↑ ... Business / Event / Time →

© Didier Schütz (DLS)

Example: a cement factory in the Caribbean islands
- Located in a Caribbean island producing bulk cement and 25kg sacks for the domestic market and international export through all the Caribbean area.
- In order to secure the supply of 25kg paper sacks, a paper plant producing printed sacks was installed on-site producing 100% of the demand (i.e. vertical integration). A just-in-time type of production was set up reducing the need for a storage area for the sacks.
- During an on-site visit, the Loss Prevention Engineer calculated the Loss Expectancy should the paper sacks factory be lost following a major fire, causing a significant impact in terms of BI for at least 12 months - the time needed for rebuilding the factory. Sales of the 25kg sacks represented about 60% of the BI (higher added values than bulk cement). So, selling only bulk cement would lead to a loss of revenue.
- There were no other factories for 25kg sacks in the group.
- They did consider the possibility of finding another supplier outside the group in case of a loss (right after the impact). However, the first delivery would take about 4 months and there would be a lot of extra costs for organizing and speeding up logistics. The margin on the sacks would decrease.
- The risk Manager decided to implement two measures:

- Maintain the equivalent of 4 months sacks consumption in different plants in the Caribbean.
- Sign a contract with an external supplier to supply at least 25-30% of normal demand so that in the case of a loss the order could easily be increased. Moreover, the supplier was chosen because it had other factories in the Caribbean but also some outside the area exposed to hurricanes. Should one factory be lost the other plants could take over.
- The direct benefit of this anticipated CP, BCP/M for the supply chain of sacks was (at least) the difference in margin between sacks and bulk products for at least 4 months.
- Moreover, selling the brand is also very important. Any interruption of the sale of sack products would allow competitors to take over the market. The cement plant could not afford the loss of market share. The financial consequences of that on a long term basis could be even greater than the loss and direct BI itself.

Example: Largest Downstream Aluminum Producer in Arabic Golf area

- Producing aluminum coils, plates and cycles for other manufacturers.
- Using 3 Rolling Mill lines involving heavy equipment with a long replacement time.
  - 12 months for a roll.
  - 24 months for a complete line (including: 8 months study, 2 months tender, 6 months manufacturing, 2 months shipping, customs clearing, 6 months installation & testing).
- Contingency Plan consisting of:
  - Having spares for each and every roll of a given type / size.
  - Strict planning of spare rolls' replacement schedule and early procurement procedure.

- "Business Continuity Management" (BCM or BCP):
  - Having a 10 year purchase option for Finished Products (corresponding to one year's production) with another downstream aluminum producer located in another country of the gulf (not competing in the same market). This would secure the major market share during the replacement of one Rolling Mill line.
- The Management was definitely risk aware, knowing the vulnerabilities of his facilities and of the supply chain in the Gulf area.

10.3.5. CP, BCP/M generating Business Opportunity

Example: A Road Maker Company (RMC) using Bitumen (3,000,000ton per annum)
- CBI exposure identified: shortage of bitumen on the market (low added value by-product from oil refinery to be re-processed in bitumen & lubricant refinery – limited numbers). Context: a very competitive environment for road construction with relatively few actors.
- Contingency Plan:
  - Decision taken by RMC: purchasing a bitumen & lubricant refinery with a contingent capacity of 1,000,000ton per annum (30% of the needs).
  - Refinery operated by the former operator of this Refinery becoming RMC staff.
- Issues:
  1. Bitumen has to be transported hot to road construction sites (generating extra costs)
  2. Low market cost of standard lubricant products (occupancy not profitable)
- Solutions:
  1. Becoming a bitumen producer for other competitor road makers (selling and or exchanging bitumen close to road construction site – thus reducing transportation costs and developing more partnerships)

2. Switching from standard lubricant processing to on-demand specialized lubricant processing (higher added value).

10.3.6. Norms, Standards and Certification

"How many people can pick up a book and find an instruction manual for their life?"
— Michael Lewis, The Big Short: Inside the Doomsday Machine

Some norms and standards about CP, BCP/M exist (i.e. ISO22301 replacing BS 25999-2). However, they just provide an organized framework based on common sense.

These norms and standards should be considered as a guideline for policy, rather than a template to stamp out identical standardized tools and procedures.

It may not be possible to provide replicable templates from one Organization to another. Each and every Organization should create its own unique set of solutions.

Some specialized consultants even propose a certification. There are about 1,000 Organizations certified worldwide, mostly in the Finance & Services sector (banks, hospitals, Public transport, airports, IT). A lot of these organizations are located in Japan and the UK.

Depending on the company, the certification process can take between 6 to 12 months prior to a pre-audit then 6 to 12 additional months for fine tuning (basically consisting of fixing all the wrong interpretations of the standard) prior to a certification audit. Then there is a regular re-certification.

The benefit of such certification is mainly to ensure that a CP, BCP/M has been developed and documented in accordance with a standardized framework. It does not, however, guarantee that the CP, BCP/M is efficiently working. When not tested and regularly updated the entire system may just become window dressing, just "paperwork for show".

10.3.7. Expect the unexpected

"I have not failed. I've just found 10,000 ways that don't work".
— Thomas Edison

As a rule of thumb, the events that are foreseen are not always the ones that occur (Murphy's Law again).

At the end of the day the BCP shows the ability of an Organization to take control of the interruption for a given identified scenario.

But not everything can be done "by the book".

However, an organization familiar with developing CP/BCPs is more likely to expect the unexpected and this grants it some ability to adjust more easily to major shifts in the market or in operating conditions.

Example 1: a forestry company in Latin America.
- This forestry company manages various plots of harvestable forests of pine wood and eucalyptus used exclusively by the nearest wood processing plant.
- Before delivery to the wood processing plant, wooden logs are stored in a yard located in the forest.
- A wild fire destroyed the main wood processing plant. 18 months were needed for reinstatement.
- In the meantime, the wooden logs could not be delivered to the wood plant. Moreover, when the logs stayed too long in the yard they became dry and could no longer be processed. This resulted in a 100% loss.
- The following BI mitigation options were investigated by the forestry company. Only option 3) was deemed as suitable:

Mitigation Options	Feasibility / Effect
1) Ask insurance to pay the whole cost (CBI)	FLEXA Property Insurance Cover (Fire, Lighting, Explosion, Aircraft) but no CBI coverage
2) Selling wooden logs to the nearest saw mill	Cannot be processed (size issue)
3) Selling wooden logs to make ships at the nearest Pulp Mill	Loss of revenue (lower margin)
4) Transporting wooden logs to another Plywood Plant	Very high Extra Costs – not profitable
5) Selling wooden logs on the market	Potential Market price collapse

Sometimes, the efficiency of the BCP has a lot to do with luck!

Example 2: 2010 an airline based in an island of the North Atlantic – Business Continuity Plan.

- 2010 eruptions of a volcano in the island creating an ash cloud over Northern Europe. All flights were suspended following an administrative decision.
- As per the planned BCP, the airline based in this island temporarily moved their base of operations from this island of the North Atlantic to an airport further south in Scotland.
- Unfortunately, this airport in Scotland also had to be closed as the ash cloud spread over a large part of Europe.

This last example about the airline based in this island of the North Atlantic during the volcano eruption shows that any BCP has its limits.

How far should an organization go? It's difficult to provide a cut and dried answer to this. The BCP should make sense and should generate some profit as detailed previously. Relocating the base of operations of this airline from this island of the North Atlantic to the Spanish Tenerife islands near Morocco would make no sense since the very purpose of this airline is to serve its nearest customers first in this island of the North Atlantic and then in its surroundings. There was no real solution in this case.

10.3.8. Aware, Adaptive, Associate

Some Organizations might be tempted to have a strange balance of power. They may be totally in favor of big brands selling Finished Products assembled by a third party with parts supplied by manufacturers. The big brand may literally suck the blood from its economic partners for whom it is often their main customer. The economic partners may be asked to conduct long and expensive Research and Development studies at their own cost without any reward other than having the right to be a supplier for such a prestigious brand.

© Franck Orset (FPO)

Some Organizations may choose to keep everything secret believing they are more advanced than all the others and they can fix any problems on their own. This overconfidence is sometimes only called into question by the Organization after a major loss has occurred. This attitude may be related to the Dunning–Kruger effect: a cognitive bias in which people incorrectly assess their cognitive abilities as greater than they actually are. The effect was discovered by two social psychologists, Dr. David Dunning and Dr. Justin Kruger. In lab experiments, they consistently found that highly unskilled people overestimated their effectiveness on a variety of measures.

The good news is that there is always an affordable learning curve so that should such an overconfident Organization survive the impact of a major loss they may have a chance to learn the lessons from their mistakes. However, the cost of this is sometimes very high.

Modern Organizations are definitively living in a connected or networked environment. This is part of the "globalization" and all the other factors described in the "ZOOG Cocktail (see section 1.3). Today there is access to a much wider market than before. Getting back to a more local market may give rise to some very difficult challenges for developing a new business model.

Such a connected and networked environment is also very critical to modern businesses enabling shifts in market or operating conditions to rapidly propagate far beyond their origins.

Non-detected shifts in market or operating conditions may cause an organization to suffer a direct financial loss but also to lose its reputation. This would have an impact on the organization worldwide but also on the nearest community such as the employees and their families, contractors, suppliers, customers.

Organizations should be able to detect any shift in its early stages of development and to come up with prompt, adequate and efficient responses.

Organizations that can intelligently and effortlessly adjust to major shifts in market or operating conditions have a competitive advantage. They are more resilient when an event occurs that was not covered in the BCP planned in advance. This 'thinking outside the box' should be routine. It's a major change in mindset involving:

- **Awareness**: developing the ability to detect any market shift and report potential resulting consequences internally. New information technologies may help to detect any critical variation in business using sensors, algorithms and some tools related to the currently primitive Artificial Intelligence. Some apps allow people to collect, analyze and share the information on line. Organizations should have a culture that encourages discussing possible problems openly.

Some big administrative-type Organizations have so many layers of hierarchy that any information reported from the bottom has very little chance of ever reaching the top. Each and every layer of hierarchy acts as a filter. In some Organizations, the corporate culture is to keep their leader happy even if it means hiding critical information. In some extreme cases, Organizations have a so called Blame Culture Management for which solving a problem consists of 'naming and shaming' the people responsible for it.

- **Adaptive** attitude: developing the ability to react effectively in case of any market shift that might have an impact on the Organization's operations. Again, this is a question of mindset. Developing embedded sensing and response capabilities inside an Organization takes time and requires full commitment from top management first. It's like playing chess. Each move leads to a new situation and a range of possible new moves. Early, fast, adequate and appropriate adaptation skill is key. When the origin is identified, some market shifts may be controlled directly with suppliers and customers. Some other market shifts may have a very remote origin. In such cases the Organization needs to take all necessary measures to curb the impact. Fast changes in procurement processes may be needed. Some markets may have to be abandoned or replaced by others. Some products may have to be re-routed or even eliminated from the range of offers.
  Some Organizations do not structurally allow for any adaptation. Internal processes, especially when certified, may lead to a certain rigidity in a given Organization. Some publicly owned Organizations can only include tenders in their procurement process rendering any emergency purchase impossible.

- **Associate** business types: establish strategies promoting collaborative action amongst network partners i.e. suppliers, any third parties involved in the operations of the Organization, customers and utility and service providers. Developing cooperative-type relationships with partners may be a big plus in a competitive landscape. Sharing knowledge with key partners about what works and what does not work is a real investment. Even in the same industry sectors, some competitors choose to share information about technology and good practices to get feedback that ultimately enhances the reliability of their own operations. Bad actors can be reported avoiding major serial losses and business interruption thanks to cutting edge modern machinery and equipment about which current knowledge is limited. We're not talking about sharing secrets here but about intelligent knowledge sharing. It can result in mutual aid and support agreements at the sectoral level in a given geographic area (i.e. Aluminum sector in the Gulf Council Countries*) or even worldwide (i.e. International Association of Ports and Harbors – IAPH*).

(*) The Gulf Aluminum Council GAC is a coordinating body that represents, promotes and protects the interests of the Aluminum industry in the Gulf. The Council's main objectives are to provide a forum for developing strategies for common issues and concerns facing the Aluminum industry in the region, and to share best practices so as to improve the efficiency of the industry.

(*) IAPH was formed in 1955 and over the last sixty years has grown into a global alliance representing over 180 member ports and 140 port-related businesses in 90 countries. The principal aim of IAPH revolves around promotion of the interests of Ports worldwide, building strong member relationships and sharing best practices among their members.

Example: 1990's – Far East Automotive Manufacturer: a very good example of a good partnership between the suppliers and their customer. Good partnership is the result of a long term development. The local cultural factor may be very important.
- A fire broke out at ASK Co's Factory in the Far East. The fire resulted in the incineration of the main source supplying 99% of crucial brake valves that a major Far East Automotive Manufacturer uses in most of its' cars.
- Only 4-hours supply of the USD 5 valve in the Far East Automotive Manufacturer plants.
- The Automotive Manufacturer had to shut down 20 auto plants in Far East (14,000 cars a day).

- Some Experts thought the Far East Automotive Manufacturer wouldn't recover for weeks.
- However, the Far East Automotive Manufacturer and its suppliers appeared to be a "Model of Cooperation".
- Suppliers and local companies rushed to the rescue.
- Within hours, they had begun taking blueprints for the valves.
- Improvising tooling systems.
- Setting up makeshift (temporary) production lines.
- NKG Co. – who made the other 1% of the Far East Automotive Manufacturer's P- valves raised production efficiency 30% by speeding up production.
- Trucks bearing the first 1,000 P-valves started arriving at the Far East Automotive Manufacturer plant almost four days after the fire.
- Five days after the fire, the Far East Automotive Manufacturer's car factories started up again.
- The Far East Automotive Manufacturer lost production of 72,000 vehicles.
- But nearly recovered the loss of output with overtime and extra shifts.
- Far East Automotive Manufacturer's Strategy After Loss was revised as follows:
  - Began an effort to trim the number of possible part variations (eventually cutting costs).
  - Sole suppliers are moving quickly to build "fail-safe mechanisms" (revamping production lines to make them more flexible or adaptable in order to easily shift to another site in case of major disaster).
  - Even stronger link between the Far East Automotive Manufacturer and the companies that pitched in during its crisis.

Example: 2000's - a Sporting Goods Company faced a reputational risk loss. This is a very good example of a fast strategic decision weighing loss of market against loss of reputation in relation to news and public opinion.

- This Sporting Goods Company was established in Western Europe and owned various shops and R&D centers. Production plants were mostly in Asia.
- Wide range of sports equipment sold i.e. for camping, horse riding, biking, but also hunting, selling guns and ammunitions
- In June 2002, an isolated man shot two people using a 22 long rifle recently purchased at the Sporting Goods Company.
- That same month an isolated man attempted to shoot the president of the country also using a 22 long rifle.
- The Company considered the potential loss of reputation as extremely serious and decided not to sell firearms anymore thus resulting in a loss of market.

Example: Following the march 2011 Earthquake and Tsunami in Tohoku and the 2016 Kumamoto quakes in Japan. This is a good example of BCP/M mutualization.

- Many manufacturers, including semiconductor makers, have developed plans for their own organizations to ensure operations continue in the event of a natural disaster.
- More than 12 semiconductor makers who each suffered major production related damages during the Kumamoto Prefecture quakes agreed to sign a pact between their businesses.
- The firms discussed how they could cooperate to continue operations in the event of disasters, after month long delays for some plants before being able to resume operations following the 2016 earthquake.
- They also decided to establish a contact system to facilitate the mutual provision of necessary parts in the wake of disaster.
- 'Production equipment uses many common components', a semiconductor industry official noted, explaining the significance of the mutual provision system.

10.4. Financing BI/CBI Residual Risk

Risk financing should not just mean purchasing capacity available on the market. This usually happens during (Re)Insurance soft market conditions that allow for very low rate insurance conditions and wide coverage. This risk is typically not paid for the carrier (i.e. (Re)Insurance market).

© Franck Orset (FPO)

Typical wrong approaches to CBI include:
- Looking for CBI Insurance coverage available on the market.
- Not being able to define the CBI coverage needs.
- Buying coverage for an unknown exposure.
- Taking the capacity offered on the market.
- Limiting Risk Management to risk mapping providing a list of 500 suppliers to (Re) Insurers (what for?).
- Not securing the supply chain.

Example: a Pharmaceutics Group – Premature Risk Transfer.
- About 90,000 tier 1 suppliers registered in a data base for Raw Material, Packaging and various consumables
- Out of these 90,000 Tier 1 suppliers:
  - 95% represent a single source: very high manufacture standard required.
  - 5% have reportedly a back-up source.
- The Business Continuity Plan of the Pharmaceutics Group consists of:

- For Tier 1 single source suppliers (#95% of 90,000): having a buffer storage on site (no duration in terms of equivalent days of production reported).
- For Tier 2 suppliers: purchasing € 900 million CBI coverage.

Premature risk transfer may even cause the (Re)Insurance market to over-react using exclusions, low sub-limits, high deductibles or (even worse) becoming risk adverse and deciding not to write any risks related to a given sector following a series of losses.

Remember that financing the risk is only the last line of defense that allows an Organization to survive the impact of a loss and to resume operations. In various cases (Re)Insurance cover may not be sufficient to save a hard-hit organization from the loss of market, reputation or any adverse conditions such as administrative closures as described in the previous sections.

It is appropriate to speak about "Residual Risk Financing" consisting of:
- Transferring the Residual Risk after all Risk Control measures (CP, BCP) have been considered and strictly enforced
- To a third party: (Re)Insurance, financial market, etc.

Residual Risk Financing is a sign of maturity for a given Organization in terms of Risk Management:
- Clearly understanding what is at stake and what are the real issues to deal with.
- Risk management actions (prevention, protection, CP, BCP/M) are assessed against risk costs (impact and consequences).
- Usually declaring that they are implementing the loss prevention recommendations submitted by the (Re)Insurance Risk Engineers for their own benefit first.

As mentioned in the previous section the wording of the BI/SI/CBI Insurance coverage when selected for "Residual Risk Transfer" should be crystal clear. Prefer standard forms (more reliable, well established, fine-tuned) than manuscript subscription forms. The usual three parties should be involved: Insured-Broker-(Re)Insurer.

Business Interruption and (Utility) Service Interruption are relatively simple concepts in terms of (Re)Insurance. The factors leading to potential financial consequences are more or less well known. The lead time of some critical modern sophisticated machinery and equipment may be longer than expected resulting in long Business Interruption Periods.

The concept of Contingent Business Interruption / Contingent Time Element can be much more complicated than expected due to the high level of uncertainty compared to BI/SI.

CBI/CTE is sometimes seen as an unpredictable quantum of Risk Transfer for which the (Re)Insurance market may not offer all necessary coverage.

11. RECOMMENDED BOOKS

Many thanks to the authors of the following books and to the one who recommended these books to me inspiring me on my journey into Business Interruption, Supply Chain and Risk Management and Risk Control in General:

The Big Short
Inside the Doomsday Machine
Michael Lewis 2010 – movie 2015

Good Strategy/Bad Strategy
The difference and why it matters
Richard Rumelt 2011

The Ethics of Belief
William Kingdon Clifford, and William James 1877

Printed in Great Britain
by Amazon